YOU'RE
PROBABLY
HAVING
A BAD
DAY

Contents

Introduction

You're probably having a bad day and thinking about giving up. Well, before you do, try and think about the hairs on your arsehole. They've been through a lot of shit, yet despite their environment they still continue to grow. So, be more like the hairs on your arsehole, deal with that shit... Well, if only it was that fucking easy! There's so much we have to deal with in life and so many things that simply get on our fucking nerves. I suppose in a way life can be compared to the hairs on your arsehole... Because it's short and full of shit!

The world we live in today can be overwhelming, stressful, and exhausting. It seems like every day there is a new challenge to overcome and the world's weight can be heavy on our shoulders. This book is a guide to help you navigate through those tough times, to remind you that you are not alone and to hopefully inspire you to keep moving forward.

Do you ever feel like life is just one big challenge after another? That no matter how hard you try, you can't seem to catch a break? Surely there's no way we were just put here to pay the bills and fucking die! Well, you're not alone. We all have bad days and sometimes it can feel like the world is against us. But what if I told you that even on your worst days, you have the power to overcome any obstacle? That you have within you the strength and resilience to keep going, no matter what life throws your way?

This guide is for anyone who has ever felt overwhelmed, stressed, or stuck in a rut. It's for those who are looking for inspiration, guidance, and practical tips on how to navigate life's challenges. Whether you're dealing with anxiety and depression, starting a business, or simply trying to find your place in the world, this guide is here to help.

In this book, we'll explore a range of topics designed to help you overcome life's challenges and find your path to success and happiness. We will delve into the current state of the world, and how it can sometimes feel like we're fighting an uphill battle. But, we will also talk about the amazing opportunities that exist all around us and how with the right mindset, we can turn even the toughest challenges into opportunities for growth and learning.

We will explore the different types of people you may encounter in your life, and how to build strong, supportive relationships that will help you on your journey. We will also discuss the role of mindfulness in finding your purpose and creating a successful business and how travel can expand your horizons and open up new possibilities.

Of course, we will also talk about some of the more difficult topics, such as anxiety and depression, and how to cope with the challenges of mental health and practical advice to help you overcome these obstacles and find joy in life.

Remember, the journey to success is not always a straight path. It can be bumpy, with twists and turns that test our resolve and make us question our decisions. But it's these moments that define us, that shape our character and make us stronger.

This book is not just about finding success or happiness, but about finding fulfilment in all aspects of your life. It's about learning to embrace the journey, even when it gets tough, and finding joy in the process. Well, just remember, the path to inner peace begins with just two words... Fuck it!
End of book, thanks for reading.

No seriously, if you're ready to take control of your life, embrace the challenges and opportunities that lie ahead and become the best version of yourself, then join me on this journey. You are capable of greatness and with the right tools and guidance, you can achieve anything you set your mind to. So, let's fucking begin...

The world today

The media bombards us with negative news every day and it can be easy to feel like the world is a terrible place. Most say the world is round, some say the world is flat but I say the world is fucked! Sometimes I feel like I need to invest in a stronger word than fuck because if aliens were to come down right now and take me away, it wouldn't be called an abduction, it would be called a fucking rescue mission.

However, the world we live in today is vastly different from the world our parents or grandparents knew. With the rise of technology, the world has become more interconnected and information is available at our fingertips. With this connectivity has come a plethora of challenges, including a constant barrage of negative news from the media. The 24-hour news cycle is always on, bombarding us with stories of violence, tragedy, disaster and for ginger people the horrific news that a heatwave is coming.

It can be overwhelming, leaving us feeling helpless and hopeless. We may feel like the world is becoming a darker, more dangerous place with each passing day. However, it's important to remember that the news often focuses on the negative, as it's what sells.

4

There is also a lot of good happening in the world too. So, sometimes I like to just kick back and watch an inspirational feel good movie, to remind myself that the world isn't so bad after all. My favourite is about a taxi driver who likes to help women from the local community get from A to B free of charge, from the kindness of his own heart. They don't have the funds for the fair so he helps them out with a free ride. There are loads of them and the journey can be viewed on camera. It doesn't take me long to watch it. Now, if that doesn't inspire you to be a better person and help you realise the world can be a better place, then I don't know what will. Some say it's fake but that's pessimism for you.

These kinds of good news stories are often overshadowed by the bad like the high cost of living, the COVID-19 pandemic, and the constant threat of global conflict. The wealth gap between the rich and the poor continues to widen, and many people are living paycheck to paycheck. This can lead to a sense of hopelessness, making it difficult to envision a brighter future.

Of course, the COVID-19 pandemic has brought its own set of challenges. Remember that part of the pandemic where it was illegal for anyone to be anywhere fucking near you... Good times!

The pandemic disrupted our daily lives, caused economic turmoil, and took a devastating toll on human life. It's forced us to confront our mortality and the fragility of our existence... However, it's also brought out the best in people, with countless acts of kindness and compassion being shown every day. Moreover, the threat of global conflict is always looming, with tensions between nations rising and the possibility of war present.

It can be frightening to think about the potential consequences of such a conflict, and it's easy to feel powerless in the face of such a daunting possibility. Despite all these challenges, it's important to remember that the world is still a beautiful and amazing place. There is so much to be grateful for, like beer and pizza.

There are so many opportunities for growth and learning and so many incredible people doing good in the world. By focusing on the positive and by taking action to create positive change, we can overcome the challenges we face and create a brighter future for ourselves and future generations. Not too bright though, it's not good for my complexion.

Nevertheless, it's important to acknowledge the challenges we face in the world today, but it's equally important to take action to address them. We can't change the world overnight, but we can make a difference in our own lives and the lives of those around us. One way to combat the negative news cycle is to limit our exposure to it. We can choose to consume news more intentionally, perhaps by reading a reliable news source once a day rather than scrolling through social media feeds all day.

It's also important to seek out positive news stories, as they can remind us that there is still good in the world. When it comes to the high cost of living, well, it's become a fucking joke hasn't it?!? Chips cost me five pounds the other day... I mean seriously, what the fuck! Chips (or fries for you American's) are just a small side. Something you like to have in addition to your meal that just gives it that extra edge. It normally comes in this fancy stupid pot or small metal fucking basket making it look like they've grown the potatoes from the garden of fucking Eden. But under no circumstance whatsoever should it cost five English pounds. It's not as if they were soaked in fucking gold!

Anyway, when it comes to the high cost of living we can take steps to manage our finances more effectively. This could mean creating a budget, cutting back on unnecessary expenses, or seeking out financial advice. It's also important to advocate for policies that address income inequality and support working families. It is a bit boring when people moan about the cost of things all the time though. Like the increase in prices of food, drink, parking and being slapped with a service charge… if you don't like it, stop coming to my fucking house!

As for the threat of global conflict, we can support diplomacy and peaceful resolution of conflicts. We can educate ourselves on the issues and advocate for policies that prioritise diplomacy over military action. We can also support organisations that work towards peace and conflict resolution.

Ultimately, taking action starts with us. It starts with acknowledging the challenges we face and then taking intentional steps to address them. It may not always be easy, but it's worth it. By creating positive change in our own lives and the world around us, we can make a difference and find fulfilment in the process.

The constant barrage of negative news can take a toll on our mental health. When we are exposed to distressing news stories regularly, it can cause us to feel anxious, helpless, and overwhelmed. It's important to recognise the impact that negative news can have on our mental health and take steps to manage it.

One way to manage the impact of negative news is to limit our exposure to it. This could mean setting boundaries around when and how often we consume news, or choosing to read only reliable news sources that are less sensationalised. We can also seek out positive news stories or stories of hope and resilience, as they can provide a counterbalance to the negativity. It's also important to take care of ourselves and prioritise self-care. This could mean taking breaks from the news or social media, just not That Ginger Fella of course!

Try doing regular exercise, practising relaxation techniques like meditation or yoga, or spending time in nature. I like nature, big fan. I've got a lot of time for a garden, specifically a beer garden, they are my favourite kind of garden. They're beautiful. You see, it's important to find what works best for us and prioritise our mental health.

Another way to manage the impact of negative news is to take action. We can channel our feelings of helplessness or anxiety into meaningful action, whether that means volunteering, donating to a cause we care about, or advocating for policy changes. By taking action, we can regain a sense of control in our lives, and feel empowered to make a positive difference.

Ultimately, it's important to recognise that while negative news can be distressing, it doesn't have to define our lives. There is always something you can do. For instance, going for a walk can improve your mental health, so I do it regularly and I end up next to an ice cream van... it really does improve my ginger day.

By managing our exposure to it, taking care of ourselves, and taking meaningful action, we can protect our mental health and find hope in a challenging world. While it's important to stay informed about the world around us, it's equally important to find balance and take care of our mental health. Consuming too much negative news can lead to a spiral of anxiety and despair, but tuning out completely can lead to feelings of disconnection and apathy. The key is to find a balance that works for us.

One way to find balance is to set boundaries around our consumption of news and social media. This could mean setting aside specific times of day to check the news or limiting the amount of time we spend scrolling through social media feeds. We can also be intentional about the sources we choose to consume, seeking out reliable news sources and limiting exposure to sensationalised or fear-mongering content.

It's important to find balance so prioritise self-care and your mental health. This could mean taking regular breaks from the news and social media, practising relaxation techniques, or seeking professional help if needed. It's important to recognise that taking care of our mental health is not a sign of weakness, but a necessary part of living a fulfilling life.

At the same time, it's important to stay engaged with the world and take meaningful action. By staying engaged and taking action, we can channel our feelings of frustration or helplessness into positive change. Finding balance can be difficult, especially after a few beers but it's about being intentional and mindful about how we consume news and engage with the world. By finding what works for us, we can protect our mental health, stay informed, and make a positive difference in the world. Instead of scrolling through social media feeds or clicking on sensationalist headlines, you could seek out reliable news sources that provide objective reporting. This would help you avoid the trap of sensationalised or fear-mongering content.

By taking care of ourselves in this way, we are better equipped to handle the stress and anxiety that can come from consuming negative news. At the same time, it's important to stay engaged with the world and take meaningful action. While it can be tempting to tune out completely in the face of overwhelming negativity, this can lead to feelings of disconnection and apathy. Instead, we can channel our frustration or helplessness into positive change. By taking care of our mental health, seeking out reliable sources of information, and staying engaged through positive action, we can find a balance that works for us and protect our well-being in the face of negativity.

Another strategy for coping with media overload is to practise gratitude. It's easy to focus on the negative aspects of the world and get bogged down by the constant flow of bad news. However, by consciously focusing on the positive things in our lives and expressing gratitude for them, we can shift our mindset and reduce our stress levels. One way to practise gratitude is to keep a gratitude journal.

Research has shown that practising gratitude can have a range of benefits for our mental health and well-being. For example, it has been linked to greater happiness, lower levels of stress and depression, and improved relationships with others.

This involves writing down three things we are grateful for each day, no matter how small they may seem. This simple exercise can help us focus on the good in our lives and increase our feelings of happiness and contentment. I'll go first... Beer, pizza, factor 50, football, fried chicken, cider, burgers, lay ins, shade, the soft contact of the female touch... Wait, I said three. Ah fuck it, list as much as you fucking what.

Engaging in activities that bring us joy and fulfilment is also important. This could mean practising a hobby, spending time with loved ones, or engaging in physical activity. Yes, that kind too. By doing things that make us feel good, we can reduce our stress levels and improve our overall well-being.

Staying informed without becoming overwhelmed is another key strategy for coping with media overload. This means being intentional about the type and amount of news we consume and taking breaks when we feel ourselves becoming overwhelmed or stressed. It's important to remember that we have control over our media consumption, and we can choose to seek out positive and uplifting news stories as well. Remember, it's okay to take breaks and step back from the constant flow of negativity. Taking care of ourselves should always be a top priority.

Additionally, the strategies mentioned above, and some practical tips can help us manage our media consumption and reduce stress. One of these is to turn off notifications on our phone or put it on silent. This can help us avoid the constant distractions and interruptions like when someone calls you without prior warning. What are you doing? Fuck off. Yes I was on my phone, yes I was scrolling and yes I could have answered very easily but I will just sit here and wait for you to hang up. I need an advance warning for these types of things, say anywhere between three to five business days.

It's also important to remember that social media is not a reflection of real life. It's easy to fall into the trap of comparing ourselves to others and feeling inadequate, but it's important to remember that people often only share their highlight reels on social media and that real life is full of ups and downs. For instance, I'm not always sarcastic and rude you know... Sometimes I sleep.

In conclusion, media overload is a real and significant challenge in today's world, and it can have a serious impact on our mental health and well-being. However, by taking practical steps to manage our media consumption, we can protect ourselves and improve our overall quality of life.

Practices for cultivating a positive mindset

I live my life by three simple rules, one is to fill what's empty, two is to empty what's full and three is to try and be happy because that's what really gets on people's fucking nerves. This is what we call mindfulness. Mindfulness is a powerful practice that can help us cultivate a more positive and resilient mindset, even in the face of the many challenges we may encounter in life.

Did you know there are over 7,000 languages, yet most people decide to talk a load of shit! Well, one effective coping strategy for dealing with this overload is to practise mindfulness. Mindfulness is about being present in the moment and observing our thoughts and feelings without judgement or attachment. One simple mindfulness practice is to take a few moments each day to focus on the positives. Find a quiet place to sit or lie down, and take a few deep, slow breaths and just remember sometimes the most spiritual thing you can do is tell someone to fuck off! My biggest regret is not telling enough people that.

Mindfulness can also be practised while doing daily tasks, such as washing dishes, having a shower or taking a dump. In addition to these practices, mindfulness meditation can also be a helpful tool for cultivating a positive mindset. Find a quiet, comfortable place to sit, and set a timer for 5-10 minutes. Close your eyes and focus on your breath, as in the first practice mentioned above. As thoughts come up, acknowledge them without judgement and bring your focus back to your breath.

By incorporating these practices into our daily lives, we can develop a more positive and resilient mindset, and cultivate greater inner peace and well-being. Life is so much better when you have a positive attitude. For example, I'm positive I'm going to go get drunk this weekend. Whether we are dealing with media overload, stress, or other challenges, mindfulness can help us stay grounded and focused on what truly matters.

Another helpful practice for cultivating a positive mindset is to engage in self-compassion. This involves treating ourselves with the same kindness and understanding that we would offer to a good friend who is going through a difficult time. Self-compassion can be especially important when we are struggling with feelings of anxiety, depression, or other mental health challenges. Instead of beating ourselves up or trying to push our feelings away, we can acknowledge our struggles and offer ourselves comfort and support.

One way to practise self-compassion is to use positive self-talk. This involves speaking to ourselves in a kind and supportive way, rather than criticising ourselves for our perceived flaws or mistakes. So, look in the mirror right now and say "Did you know a whale's anus can stretch up to forty inches wide, making it the second biggest arsehole in the world, behind you". Wait... No, that's not self-compassion. However, you can say this to someone else and that counts as mindfulness.

You can try to engage in self-care activities that promote relaxation, well-being, and enjoyment. Ultimately, cultivating a positive mindset involves making a conscious effort to focus on the good in our lives, even when things are difficult. By practising mindfulness, self-compassion, and other positive mindset techniques, we can develop greater resilience and inner strength and navigate life's challenges with greater ease and grace.

Another helpful practice for cultivating a positive mindset is to set goals and work towards them. This can give us a sense of purpose and direction in our lives, and help us stay motivated and engaged. When setting goals, it's important to make them specific, measurable, achievable, relevant and time-bound. This is often referred to as the SMART framework. By setting SMART goals, we can break down big, intimidating goals into smaller, more manageable steps and track our progress along the way. Or you can use the GINGE framework:

Grab a beer.
Indulge in some libation.
Neck a few more beers.
Get loads of pizza.
Eat the fucking lot!

I mean, I'm not sure it's going to help with setting goals but it sounds like a good night.

Of course, it's important to remember that cultivating a positive mindset is an ongoing process, and there will be times when we struggle or face setbacks. However, by practising mindfulness, self-compassion, gratitude, and goal-setting, we can build resilience and develop a more positive outlook on life.

People

All this "try and be positive" stuff and "focus on the good" is tough though isn't it? I bet everyday you wake up hoping to have a good day and try to be as positive as a Sunday morning pregnancy test but the trouble is there are three things guaranteed in life: Death, taxes and people getting on your fucking nerves!

Apparently, there are over 7 trillion nerves in the human body, well some people manage to get on every single fucking one of them. People are complex and come in all shapes and sizes, and not everyone is going to be your cup of tea or pint of beer. You see, people give you a reason to drink. You don't even need a fucking reason to drink, all you need is a glass but people seem to intensify that need.

Let's explore different personalities, how to deal with difficult people, and how to build meaningful relationships. In life, we come across many different types of people, each with a unique personality, background, and experiences. A type of person we may encounter is the negative one. I may be coming across as quite negative, but I'm not negative, I encourage people all the time... Normally to fuck off! But I think that's great advice.

A negative person is the type who always sees the glass as half empty. I don't see the glass half empty or half full, I see that there's obviously fucking room for more! Anyway, this person is quick to complain about anything and everything. It's important to remember that their negativity is not a reflection of you or anything you have done, but rather a reflection of their internal struggles.

On the other hand, we have the positive one who always sees the good in everything and everyone. While their optimism can be contagious, it's fucking annoying and it's important to remember that they may not always see the reality of a situation and may need some grounding in the facts.

Then there's the know it all who always has an opinion on everything and is quick to share their knowledge, whether it's asked for or fucking not. I know, these people are what we call a fucking nightmare! While their expertise can be valuable, it's important to remember that everyone has something to contribute and listening to others can lead to more well-rounded solutions.

We also have the people-pleaser who is always trying to make everyone happy and avoid conflict at all costs. While their intentions are good, it's important to remember that it's impossible to please everyone, you're not cake. Sometimes conflict is necessary for growth and progress.

Then we have the independent spirit who marches to the beat of their drum and doesn't conform to societal norms. While their individuality is admirable, it's important to remember that working together and considering the perspectives of others can lead to more successful outcomes.

We encounter different types of people every day, and each person is unique. It's important to understand that everyone has their own story, experiences and beliefs that shape who they are. When we take the time to understand and appreciate these differences, we can build stronger connections and more meaningful relationships. Although this can be tough can't it? Especially when we live in a universe scientists say is made up of electrons, protons and neutrons. But I guess they forgot about the fucking morons!

Another type of person we often encounter is the pessimist. Pessimists tend to focus on the negative aspects of a situation and may have a difficult time seeing the positive. These people need to shove a lamp up their arse, so they can lighten the fuck up! They may be quick to criticise and complain and their negative energy can be draining.

On the other hand, we have optimists who tend to focus on the positive aspects of a situation. They see challenges as opportunities and approach life with a glass half full mentality. Optimists can be a source of inspiration and positivity for those around them.

Then there are the realists who try to see things as they are, without sugarcoating or exaggerating. They tend to be grounded and practical and may provide a balanced perspective to a situation.

Of course, these are just a few examples of the many different types of people we encounter in our lives. You may find it inconceivable that women aren't able to conceive via anal sex, as there are too many arseholes in this world for it not to be true. However, it's important to remember that each person is unique and complex and there is no one-size-fits-all approach to understanding them.

Like cancel culture and all the snowflakes in the modern world that make it seem as if we're living at the north fucking pole! Did you know there are over 10,000 nerve endings in the clitoris? Yet it's still not as sensitive as some fucking people! Cancel culture has become a ubiquitous term in our current social and political climate. It refers to the practice of publicly calling out individuals or organisations for behaviour or actions deemed inappropriate or offensive, with the aim of holding them accountable for their actions. While some see it as a necessary tool for promoting social justice, others view it as a form of censorship and mob justice that can have severe consequences for those who are "cancelled".

The rise of social media has played a significant role in the proliferation of cancel culture. With the ability to share information and opinions instantly and widely, individuals and groups can easily mobilise and call attention to instances of wrongdoing or offensive behaviour. While this can lead to positive change, it can also result in online harassment, cyberbullying, and the spread of misinformation. One of the challenges with cancel culture is that it often operates in a binary manner, with little room for nuance or discussion.

Individuals are either "cancelled" or they are not with little consideration given to the complexity of human behaviour and the potential for growth and redemption. This can lead to a lack of empathy and understanding, as well as a disregard for due process and the presumption of innocence. Moreover, cancel culture often comes with severe consequences for those who are targeted. This can include losing one's job, being ostracised from one's community, and enduring online harassment and threats. These consequences can have long-lasting effects on individuals and their families, and can create a chilling effect on free speech and open dialogue.

On one hand, some argue that it's a necessary tool for holding people accountable for their actions and promoting social justice. On the other hand, others argue that it's a form of censorship and can have severe consequences for individuals who are "cancelled". While it is important to hold individuals and organisations accountable for their actions, it is equally important to consider the broader context in which those actions occurred and to allow for the possibility of growth and redemption. Ultimately, the question of whether cancel culture is a force for good or a form of censorship is a complex and nuanced one, and one that requires ongoing discussion and dialogue.

Supporters of cancel culture argue that it's a necessary tool for holding people accountable for their actions. They argue that calling out bad behaviour is essential for promoting social justice and creating a safer, more equitable society. In this view, cancel culture is a form of activism that can bring about positive change.

Opponents of cancel culture, however, argue that it's a form of censorship that can have severe consequences for individuals who are "cancelled". They argue that cancel culture can be driven by mob mentality and can lead to individuals being unfairly targeted and punished for minor offences. In this view, cancel culture is a threat to free speech and can have a chilling effect on open and honest dialogue.

While it's important to hold people accountable for their actions, it's also essential to ensure that the consequences are proportionate to the offence. Cancel culture can be a powerful tool for promoting social justice, but it can also be used as a weapon to silence dissenting opinions and punish individuals for minor infractions. One of the challenges with cancel culture is that it often operates in a black-and-white, all-or-nothing manner. People are either "cancelled"; or they aren't, with little room for nuance or discussion. While there are certainly cases where cancel culture has been used to promote social justice and hold individuals accountable for their actions, there are also cases where it has been used to silence dissent and punish individuals for minor infractions.

As a society, we must continue to have open and honest conversations about cancel culture and its impact on our collective well-being as it often operates in a way that assumes that people cannot change or learn from their mistakes. It is important to hold individuals accountable for their actions but it is equally important to provide them with opportunities for growth and redemption. People should not be defined by their worst moments and it is possible for individuals to learn from their mistakes and become better people. Unless you put pineapple on pizza... unforgivable.

Another concern is the potential for cancel culture to be weaponised for personal gain or to settle personal scores. In some cases, people may use cancel culture as a way to gain social capital or to target individuals they do not like. This can result in innocent people being unfairly targeted and punished for actions that do not warrant such severe consequences.

Cancel culture is a complex and controversial topic that raises important questions about accountability, free speech and social justice. While there are certainly cases where cancel culture has been used effectively to hold individuals accountable for their actions, there are many cases where it has been used to stifle free speech and punish individuals unfairly.

So, what we should do is stop this culture that when someone says they're offended, they expect us to give a fuck. If the 99% of people who aren't offended by anything and everything stop giving a fuck about the 1% that are then the world will be a much happier place. So, switch to not giving a fuck today, it'll be the best decision you ever make.

Guidance on starting a business

You're probably having a bad day and thinking about giving up, well before you do just remember that Bill Gates made his first million when he was just 26 and Steve Jobs made his first million when he was just 23... so yeah, you should probably just give up.

I kid. I kid. But, I bet you are actually having a bad day and you probably have two milestones when you're at work. Lunch and fucking leaving! Well, did you know that if you text your manager right now "Go fuck yourself", you don't have to go to work tomorrow? I know, shocker.

Well, for the majority of our life we are going to need to work so you need to try and enjoy what you do for a living. You need to wake up on a Monday morning excited about the week ahead. This is a real challenge and it makes you think, can you believe we used to moan about having to go to school? Monday to Friday 9am to 3.30pm, half term holidays, Christmas holidays, Easter holidays, summer holidays, being with our mates every single day, no bills to pay and no responsibilities... we were living the dream and we didn't even fucking know it!

If you're not enjoying your job and you constantly dream of the retirement age being halved because you've simply fucking had enough, then you may be thinking about starting your own business.

Starting a business can be a daunting task and sometimes you may need guidance to find purpose, a meaning to your work and help on how to stay motivated when the going gets tough. Many successful entrepreneurs practise visualisation techniques, such as imagining themselves achieving their goals and manifesting their desired outcomes. Some seek spiritual guidance to connect with like-minded individuals who share the same values and beliefs. However, identifying your values and purpose in business is an essential step toward creating a successful and fulfilling entrepreneurial journey.

When you are clear about your values and purpose, it becomes easier to make decisions, stay motivated, and create a strong brand identity. Values are the beliefs and principles that guide your behaviour and decision-making. They are the foundation of your business and reflect what you stand for. For example, if you value transparency and honesty, your business practices and communication should reflect those values.

Purpose, on the other hand, is the reason behind what you do. It is the driving force that motivates you to start and continue your business. Your purpose should be aligned with your values and should be something that inspires and excites you. It could be to solve a problem in your community, to create a better future for your family, or to contribute to a cause that you are passionate about. Identifying your values and purpose in business can be a challenging process, but it is essential for creating a strong foundation for your venture.

Here are some steps to help you identify your values and purpose:

1. Reflect on your values.
Start by reflecting on your values and what is important to you. Write down a list of values that resonate with you and prioritise them.

2. Connect your values to your business.
Once you have identified your values, think about how they can be reflected in your business practices. For example, if you value sustainability, you can prioritise eco-friendly products or services.

3. Identify your strengths.
Think about your strengths and how they can contribute to

your business. This could be a particular skill set or area of expertise.

4. Determine your mission.
Your mission statement should articulate your purpose and the reason behind your business. It should be concise and easy to understand.

5. Create a vision.
Your vision should outline the long-term goals of your business and what you hope to achieve. It should be ambitious but realistic.

It is important to regularly reflect on your values and purpose and ensure that they are aligned with your business practices. When you are clear about your values and purpose, it can inspire others to support your vision and help your business succeed.

However, it is important to understand what motivates you, what you stand for, and what you want to achieve through your business. Without a clear sense of purpose, it is easy to get sidetracked and lose sight of what you are trying to achieve. Personally I'm motivated by winning, as I fucking hate losing. The only thing I've actually enjoyed losing was my virginity. Now, that was a great 42 seconds... But losing at bowling, pool, fantasy football, darts, shuffleboard, table tennis, air hockey, any video games, etc, doesn't just ruin my day, it ruins my fucking week. I don't care if you're a small child, I am not letting you win. Fuck that!

Anyway, back to values... One effective way to identify your values and purpose is to take a step back and reflect on your personal beliefs, principles, examine your business goals and objectives.

What drives you?
What are the core values that you hold dear?
What do you stand for?
What do you want to achieve through your business?
What do you hope to accomplish through your business?
What do you want your business to be known for?
What do you want to contribute to the world through your business?

Once you have a clear understanding of your values and purpose, it is important to integrate these into every aspect of your business. This means aligning your business practices and decisions with your values and purpose and communicating this to your customers, employees, and stakeholders. For example, if one of your core values is sustainability, you may choose to implement environmentally friendly practices in your business operations. If your purpose is to make a positive impact on your community, you may choose to donate a portion of your profits to local charities or volunteer your time to community initiatives. Or maybe you like to keep your local chinese and indian takeaway in business? Me too, always happy to help.

By integrating your values and purpose into your business, you not only create a more meaningful and fulfilling experience for yourself but also attract like-minded individuals who share your values and purpose. This can lead to more productive and fulfilling partnerships and collaborations. Nevertheless, think about what motivates you, what makes you happy, and what you are passionate about. Your values and purpose should align with these things.

Another way to identify your values and purpose in business is to create a mission statement. A mission statement is a concise statement that defines the purpose of your business and what you hope to achieve. It should reflect your values and purpose and guide your decision-making processes.

Once you have identified your values and purpose, it is important to communicate them effectively to your team. This will help them understand the direction of the business and make decisions that align with your values and purpose. It is also important to revisit and revise your values and purpose as your business evolves. Your values and purpose may change over time as your business grows and you gain new experiences and insights.

In conclusion, identifying your values and purpose in business is crucial for success and satisfaction. It helps you stay motivated, make better decisions, and communicate effectively with your team and stakeholders. Don't forget to take the time to reflect on your personal experiences and beliefs, create a mission statement, and communicate your values and purpose effectively to ensure that your business aligns with your values and purpose. I'll tell you one thing I forgot to do, I forgot to go to the gym again today. That's 7 years in a fucking row... what a shame!

Setting goals and staying motivated in business

Staying motivated is absolutely key and once you have a clear understanding of your values and purpose in business, setting goals can be the next step to achieving success. Setting realistic and measurable goals can help you to stay focused and motivated in your business journey. When setting goals, it's important to consider the SMART criteria - Specific, Measurable, Achievable, Relevant, and Time-bound.

Did you know, the most remote place on earth lies in the south pacific ocean and it's called Point Nemo. No land and no people. In fact it's so isolated at Point Nemo that if you were to go there and the international space station was orbiting above, the astronauts would be the closest people to you. That makes me happy, that's what motivates me. A boat! I'd love to own a boat, I would call it The Ginger Surfer. Or maybe Ship Happens, Aquaholic, Netfish & Chill, or She Got the House... I would be out on my boat all the time just singing "Row, row, row your boat, gently the fuck away from me". It would feel fantastic.

Anyway, your goals should be clear and specific so that you know exactly what you want to achieve. They should also be measurable so that you can track your progress and know when you have achieved them. Additionally, your goals should be achievable and relevant to your overall purpose and values and should be time-bound, with a specific deadline.

To stay motivated in your business, it's also important to regularly review and revise your goals. This can help you to stay on track and make any necessary adjustments to your plan. Celebrating small successes along the way can also help to keep you motivated and focused on your ultimate goals.

Another helpful strategy for staying motivated is to find an accountability partner or mentor who can provide support and guidance along the way. This person can help to keep you accountable and motivated and can offer valuable insights and advice based on their own experiences.

Try to take care of your physical and mental well-being as this is crucial for staying motivated in business. By following these tips and staying true to your values and purpose, you can stay motivated and achieve success in your business endeavours. Goals give you a clear direction of where you want to go and what you want to achieve.

However, setting goals is not enough. You need to stay motivated to achieve them. I know this can be challenging, especially when you encounter setbacks or face obstacles. Sometimes life will try and fuck you and you just have to roll over, change positions and try to enjoy the ride. Well, here are some tips to help you set goals and stay motivated in business:

1. Set SMART goals.
Your goals should be Specific, Measurable, Attainable, Relevant, and Time-bound. Setting SMART goals makes them more achievable and helps you stay on track.

2. Break down your goals into smaller tasks.
When you break down your goals into smaller, more manageable tasks, you'll be able to see your progress and feel more motivated.

3. Stay focused on your "why".
Your "why" is the reason you started your business in the first place. When you stay focused on your "why", it can help you stay motivated and committed to your goals.

4. Celebrate your successes.
Celebrating your successes, no matter how small, can help

keep you motivated and build momentum toward achieving your goals.

5. Find an accountability partner.

Having someone to hold you accountable can help keep you motivated and on track. Consider finding a mentor, joining a mastermind group, or working with a business coach.

6. Take breaks and prioritise self-care.

Running a business can be stressful and overwhelming. Taking breaks and prioritising self-care can help you stay motivated and prevent burnout.

7. Keep learning and growing.

Continuing to learn and grow in your industry can keep you motivated and inspired. Attend conferences, read books, and take courses to stay up-to-date on industry trends and best practices.

Setting goals and staying motivated in business are essential for long-term success. By setting SMART goals, breaking them down into smaller tasks, staying focused on your "why", celebrating your successes, finding an accountability partner, prioritising self-care, and continuing to learn and grow, you can achieve your goals and stay motivated along the way.

However, another important factor in staying motivated is celebrating your successes along the way. When you reach a milestone or accomplish a goal, take the time to acknowledge and celebrate your achievements. This can be as simple as treating yourself to something you enjoy, like a nice dinner or a relaxing day off. Celebrating your successes can help you stay motivated and keep pushing toward your next goal.

It's also important to stay connected to your "why". Remind yourself of the reasons why you started your business and why you're passionate about it. This can help reignite your motivation and keep you focused on your goals. Use tools and systems to help you stay on track and manage your time effectively. This can include things like calendars, to-do lists, and project management software. By staying organised and focused, you can avoid feeling overwhelmed and stay motivated to tackle your tasks and goals.

In conclusion, setting goals and staying motivated is essential for business success. By identifying your values and purpose, breaking down your goals into actionable steps, celebrating your successes, staying connected to your "why"; and staying organised and focused, you can stay motivated and achieve your business goals. Remember to take breaks and take care of yourself along the way to avoid burnout and stay motivated for the long haul. Never see yourself as a failure. You most likely started out life as a shoulder massage and now look, you've come a long way.

Overcoming self-doubt and imposter syndrome

You're probably having a bad day and maybe you're thinking you're not good enough. Well, just remember the only thing standing in the way of you and your dreams is your personality, lack of talent and general appearance…

Again, I kid. You see overcoming self-doubt and imposter syndrome is a significant challenge for many people who are starting a business. Even if you have experience or expertise in a particular area, you may feel like you are not qualified enough or that you do not have the necessary skills to succeed. This can lead to feelings of anxiety, stress, and self-doubt, which can ultimately hold you back from achieving your goals.

One effective way to overcome self-doubt and imposter syndrome is to not give a fuck. Did you know that studies show that stress is caused by giving a fuck? Well, what if I told you that you could save 100% on stress by switching to not giving a fuck. You think you're not good enough… who gives a fuck. You believe you're not worthy… who gives a fuck. You think you shouldn't be here… who gives a fuck. Switch to not giving a fuck today to improve your mental well-being and reduce stress.

It'll be the best decision you ever make because let me tell you something for free, well it's not for free as you just paid for this book and thanks for doing so by the way, appreciate it. Anyway, let me tell you that you are good enough, you are worthy and you should be here, so try and focus on your strengths and achievements. This can help you build confidence in your abilities and recognise that you are capable of achieving success.

Take time to reflect on your past accomplishments and remind yourself of the skills and experience that you bring to the table. Instead of dwelling on your shortcomings or failures, make a list of your accomplishments and the skills that you have developed. This can help shift your focus to the positive aspects of yourself and your business.

Another helpful strategy is to seek out support and advice from others. Talking to mentors or other entrepreneurs who have gone through similar experiences can be incredibly valuable, as they can provide guidance and insight that can help you overcome obstacles and build your confidence. Surrounding yourself with a supportive network of friends, family, and mentors can provide you with the encouragement, reassurance and advice that you need to help you push through your doubts, believe in your entrepreneurial vision and abilities, and provide a valuable source of motivation and inspiration to achieve your goals.

It is also essential to develop a growth mindset, which involves viewing challenges and failures as opportunities for learning and growth. Instead of seeing setbacks as evidence of your inadequacy, try to see them as opportunities to develop new skills or learn from your mistakes.

It is crucial to practise self-care and prioritise your mental health. Starting a business can be a stressful and challenging endeavour, and it is important to take care of yourself both physically and mentally. This might involve setting aside time for exercise, meditation, or other self-care activities, as well as seeking out professional support if needed. By focusing on your strengths, seeking out support, developing a growth mindset, and prioritising self-care, you can overcome self-doubt and imposter syndrome and achieve success in your business endeavours.

Remember that self-doubt is a common experience, but it does not have to hold you back from achieving your goals. With the right mindset and support, you can overcome these challenges and realise your full potential. Imposter syndrome can affect anyone, regardless of their experience or expertise, particularly entrepreneurs starting their own businesses. It is characterised by a persistent self-doubt, fear of being exposed as a fraud or feeling inadequate despite evidence of one's competence or qualifications needed to succeed in their endeavours.

This self-doubt can be crippling, leading to anxiety, stress and even depression. However, there are ways to overcome imposter syndrome and build confidence in yourself and your abilities. One of the most effective ways to overcome imposter syndrome is to recognise that you are not alone. Many successful entrepreneurs have experienced imposter syndrome at some point in their careers, and acknowledging this can help you realise that your feelings are normal and not a reflection of your actual abilities.

Ultimately, it is important to remember that failure is a natural part of the entrepreneurial journey. Instead of fearing failure, embrace it as an opportunity to learn and grow. By reframing failure as a learning experience, you can build resilience and become more confident in your abilities. For entrepreneurs, imposter syndrome can be particularly challenging, as starting a business requires a lot of risk-taking and self-confidence. However, there are ways to overcome imposter syndrome and build the confidence necessary to succeed in business.

Entrepreneurs can benefit from adjusting their mindset about failure. Instead of seeing failures as proof of their inadequacy, entrepreneurs can view them as opportunities for reflection and improvement. By adopting a growth mindset, entrepreneurs can focus on the progress they are making rather than dwelling on their perceived shortcomings.

In summary, imposter syndrome is a common challenge faced by many entrepreneurs. However, by acknowledging accomplishments, seeking support, adopting a growth mindset, and taking care of mental and physical health, entrepreneurs can overcome self- doubt and build the confidence necessary to succeed in business.

So if you're looking for inspiration and motivation then look no further, I'm your guy. After all my blood type is B positive… Lies, I don't have blood, or a soul or the expertise to find the G-Spot, but what I do have is enough inspiration and motivation to at least make you feel confident in yourself. Now, look outside and find a tree then look at the branches, most look weak right? Well, if a bird were to sit on one of those weak branches, it wouldn't be scared because the bird's trust is not within the branch itself but in the strength of it's own wings… I know. So, be like the bird, trust your strengths and now get moving you lazy fuck!

Developing a personal brand for your business

Developing a personal brand and marketing your business are essential steps toward establishing a successful venture. If you're not lucky enough to be ginger and play on that until you go bald or turn into a silver fox, you're going to have to come up with something. A personal brand is the unique identity of a person that distinguishes them from others. It reflects their values, beliefs, and the way they do business.

Similarly, marketing is the process of promoting products or services to potential customers. To develop a personal brand, it is important to identify what sets you apart from your competitors. This could be your skills, experience, or unique perspective. Once you have identified your unique selling proposition, you can start building your brand around it.

One effective way of building a personal brand is through content creation. By sharing valuable content on social media, blogs, or podcasts, you can establish yourself as an authority in your field. This can help you attract a following of people who are interested in what you have to offer. Marketing your business involves identifying your target audience and understanding their needs and preferences. This can be done through market research, surveys, or focus groups. Once you have a clear understanding of your target audience, you can tailor your marketing efforts to appeal to them. One effective marketing strategy is to use social media platforms to promote your products or services. By creating engaging content and engaging with your followers, you can build a loyal customer base. Another effective marketing strategy is to partner with other businesses or influencers in your industry. This can help you reach a wider audience and establish credibility in your field.

Developing a personal brand and marketing your business are essential steps toward building a successful venture. By identifying your unique selling proposition and understanding your target audience, you can create a brand that resonates with your customers. Through effective marketing strategies like content creation and social media marketing, you can attract and retain a loyal customer base.

Try doing some market research on your brand. It can be very valuable but it might not always go according to plan. For instance, last weekend I asked one hundred women what they prefer to wear in bed. Well, you'd be surprised to know the most common answer is… what the hell are you doing behind my curtains?!? Get out of my house! I know, how rude.

Anyway, your brand is the image and reputation that you create for yourself and your business. It is the way you present yourself to your target audience and the world. In today's world of social media and online marketing building a personal brand is more critical than ever. It is through your brand that people will get to know you, your values, and your business. To develop a personal brand, start by identifying your unique qualities and strengths.

What makes you stand out?
What are your values?
What are your beliefs?
And what are your passions?

Think about how you want to be perceived by your target audience and what kind of impression you want to make. Once you have a clear idea of your brand, you can begin to develop your marketing strategy. Your marketing strategy should be based on your personal brand and target audience.

Consider the various online platforms available to you as establishing a strong online presence is crucial. This includes social media, email marketing, content marketing, a professional website that showcases your brand and optimising your content for search engines so that potential clients can find you easily.

Determine which platforms are best suited for your business and create a plan to reach your target audience. It is also essential to stay consistent with your branding. Ensure that your brand image and message are consistent across all platforms and marketing materials. This consistency will help to build trust and credibility with your audience.

Your brand can also be used to network and build relationships with other professionals in your industry. Attend industry events, conferences, and seminars, and use these opportunities to connect with others and build your brand. Remember that building a personal brand is an ongoing process. Continuously evaluate your brand and adjust your marketing strategy as needed. By taking the time to develop a strong personal brand, you can establish yourself as a leader in your industry and grow your business.

One way to establish and market your brand is by creating content that showcases your expertise and knowledge in your industry. This can be done through writing blog posts, creating videos, or hosting webinars. By sharing your insights and perspectives, you can build trust with your audience and position yourself as a thought leader in your field. Networking is also a valuable tool for marketing your business and building your brand. Attending industry events, joining professional associations, and connecting with peers on social media can all help you expand your network and make valuable connections. Building relationships with potential clients, partners, and collaborators can open up new opportunities for your business.

It's important to have a clear understanding of your target audience and how to effectively communicate with them. This includes understanding their needs and pain points, developing messaging that resonates with them, and using the right channels to reach them. By effectively communicating with your audience, you can build a loyal following and grow your business. Once you have developed your brand, the next step is to market your business effectively. Marketing is crucial to the success of any business, as it helps you to reach potential customers and communicate the value of your products or services.

Here are some effective marketing strategies to consider:

1. Social Media Marketing.
Social media platforms are powerful tools for promoting your business. They allow you to connect with your target audience, build brand awareness, and generate leads. Make sure to create a strong social media presence by posting engaging content regularly, interacting with your followers, and using paid advertising to reach a wider audience.

2. Content Marketing.

Content marketing involves creating and sharing valuable content, such as blog posts, videos, and infographics, that educates and informs your target audience. This approach can help you to establish your business as an authority in your industry and build trust with potential customers.

3. Email Marketing.

Email marketing involves sending targeted emails to your subscriber list to promote your business. This approach can be highly effective when done correctly, as it allows you to reach people who have already expressed an interest in your products or services. Make sure to create personalised and engaging emails that provide value to your subscribers.

4. Influencer Marketing.

Influencer marketing involves partnering with influential people in your industry to promote your business. This approach can be highly effective as it allows you to tap into the audience of the influencer and leverage their credibility and reach to promote your business.

5. Networking.

Networking involves building relationships with other professionals in your industry and attending events to promote your business. This approach can be highly effective as it allows you to connect with potential customers and partners, and build your reputation in your industry. In conclusion, marketing your business effectively is crucial to its success.

By leveraging the above marketing strategies, you can reach potential customers, establish your brand as an authority, and build trust with your target audience. Remember to focus on providing value and creating engaging content, and always be open to trying new marketing approaches to find what works best for your business.

Balancing work and life to prevent burnout

Does it feel like it's been one of those weeks for about nine fucking years? Well, balancing work and life is an essential aspect of maintaining a healthy and fulfilling lifestyle. When starting a business, it can be easy to become consumed by work, leaving little time for other important aspects of life, such as family, friends, and self-care. However, neglecting these areas can lead to burnout, decreased productivity, and even negative physical and mental health outcomes.

We live in a universe where there are billions of galaxies, trillions of stars and quadrillions of planets, yet we live on one where we have to work a forty hour fucking week. Splendid. However, just like a bit of backdoor penetration here comes some deep shit. By the time we get there, retirement age will be seventy and life expectancy eighty, you'll work fifty to sixty years to enjoy a mere fucking decade and that doesn't sit right on my ginger watch. So, we should enjoy the moment, live in the present because quite simply tomorrow is never guaranteed.

Therefore, it is crucial to implement strategies to balance work and life effectively. The first step in achieving this balance is setting realistic expectations. Entrepreneurs are often filled with ambition and drive, which can lead to overworking and unrealistic expectations for themselves. It is crucial to understand that starting a business is a process that takes time, and success may not happen overnight. Setting achievable goals and timelines can help reduce stress and prevent burnout.

Another essential aspect of balancing work and life is creating a schedule and sticking to it. This involves setting aside dedicated time for work, personal responsibilities, and self-care activities. By creating a structured schedule, entrepreneurs can ensure they have time for all important aspects of their life, reducing the likelihood of becoming overwhelmed.

Balancing work and life is essential for entrepreneurs to prevent burnout, maintain productivity, and achieve long-term success. By setting realistic expectations, creating a schedule, setting boundaries, practising self-care, and seeking support, entrepreneurs can effectively balance work and life and enjoy a fulfilling and healthy lifestyle.

To prevent burnout, it is essential to find a healthy balance between work and personal life. Without adequate rest and self-care, individuals can easily become overworked, stressed, and emotionally exhausted. Finding a balance between the two is not always easy, especially for business owners who have to wear many hats and juggle multiple responsibilities. One way to prevent burnout is by creating a schedule and sticking to it. By blocking out time for work and personal life, individuals can prioritise their tasks and ensure they have time for both. It is also crucial to establish boundaries, such as not checking emails or taking work calls during personal time. This helps to create separation and reduce the risk of burnout.

Another important aspect of work-life balance is self-care. This includes engaging in activities that promote physical, emotional, and mental well-being, such as exercise, hobbies, and spending time with loved ones. It is essential to prioritise self-care just as much as work-related tasks, as it can significantly impact an individual's overall health and happiness.

Finding a balance between work and personal life requires a conscious effort to prioritise one's well-being. Another helpful strategy is delegating tasks and responsibilities to others when possible. This can include outsourcing certain aspects of the business or hiring additional staff to lighten the workload. It is important to remember that burnout is a real and serious issue, and taking proactive steps to prevent it is essential for both personal and professional success.

There are some amazing stories out there, from the woman who was sole survivor of a plane crash and survived 11 days alone in the Amazon rainforest, to the man who survived 14 months alone in a small fishing boat drifting 7,000 miles across the Pacific Ocean. They survived the impossible, but do you know what the greatest survival story of all time is? You! When you make it through the working fucking week. What a warrior! You probably had a bad week being overworked, underpaid and you probably had to deal with more shit than a fucking sewer! So, you deserve a break, maybe a holiday, because the only place you've been flying to recently is off the fucking handle. So, try and have a good time and let your hair down, as it won't last long... that's what she said.

Now, always remember that even if you make loads of money, exercise, sleep well, drink plenty of water and eat healthy food, you will still die... So, you still need to enjoy your fucking self!

Travelling and the eventuality of death

Speaking of death, as cliche as it is, life is so short and we should make the fucking most of it. Travelling is a great way to expand our horizons and gain new experiences. I love to travel. I love the airport, it's the only place you can start drinking at 6am and it is perfectly fucking acceptable.

Travelling can be an amazing and transformative experience, allowing us to discover new places, cultures, and perspectives. However, it can also serve as a reminder of the fragility of life and the inevitability of death. This paradoxical nature of travel makes it all the more valuable, as it encourages us to embrace the present moment and live our lives to the fullest.

One of the most powerful aspects of travel is its ability to break us out of our routines and challenge our assumptions. When we visit a new place, we are forced to confront unfamiliar customs, foods, languages, and social norms. This can be both exciting and daunting, but it always offers the opportunity to broaden our horizons and expand our understanding of the world.

At the same time, travelling can also be a humbling experience, reminding us of our mortality and the fleeting nature of life. Whether we are hiking in the mountains, lounging on a tropical beach, or exploring a bustling city, we are always acutely aware of the fact that our time in that place is limited. This can be a sobering realisation, but it also motivates us to make the most of our experiences and cherish each moment.

Travelling can also help us gain perspective on our lives and priorities. When we step out of our everyday routine and environment, we can see things from a different angle and re-evaluate our goals and values. This can be a powerful tool for personal growth and development, as it allows us to identify areas where we may be stuck or unfulfilled, and make changes to align more closely with our true desires and aspirations.

We also like to get away to forget, especially about the working week, specifically Monday. Now, we all know light travels faster than sound, which is why some people appear bright until you speak to them, but did you know there's only one thing that travels faster than light? The fucking weekend! So much so that if Monday was a gender, then it would be a man, because it comes way too fucking quickly!

However, as with any endeavour, travel can also have its downsides. It can be expensive, stressful, time-consuming, and it may not always live up to our expectations. The more we travel, the more we may become aware of the disparities and injustices that exist in the world, and this can be a challenging realisation to grapple with. Nevertheless, it is precisely these challenges and complexities that make travel such a valuable and an enriching experience.

By confronting the realities of life and death, we are forced to acknowledge the impermanence of all things and appreciate the moments we have while we have them. And by embracing the uncertainties and difficulties of travel, we can grow in ways we never imagined, becoming more resilient, compassionate, and open-minded human beings.

Travelling exposes you to different cultures, languages, and ways of life. It broadens your perspective, challenges your assumptions, and opens your mind to new possibilities. But beyond the adventure and excitement, travelling can also teach us an important lesson about life, that it is short and precious.

The reality of our mortality can be a difficult concept to accept, but it is an important one to keep in mind as we go about our daily lives. We often get caught up in the routine of work, school, and other responsibilities, forgetting that our time on this earth is finite. Travelling can remind us of this fact by presenting us with new experiences and opportunities that may not come around again. It can inspire us to make the most of our time and appreciate the people and experiences that bring us joy.

Furthermore, travelling can also teach us about the beauty of life in the face of death. When we encounter different cultures and traditions, we are exposed to different perspectives on life, death, and the afterlife. Some cultures celebrate death as a natural part of the cycle of life, while others view it as a transition to another world. In either case, travelling can help us appreciate the value of life and the importance of cherishing the time we have with loved ones.

Going away just makes us happy doesn't it. Talking of happiness, did you know Finland has been named the happiest country in the world six times in a row. I want to know what the fuck they are drinking because I want some, it seems to be working. Last time around, the UK was named 19th on that list which is remarkably high considering you can't get a doctors appointment because they're overworked and underpaid, the trains haven't worked since 1992, food and energy prices are as high as a fucking stoner and the country is run by corrupt, dishonest, out of touch fucking morons. People say I should look on the bright side… Look on the bright side?!? I can't, I'm ginger, if I look on the bright side I will fucking burn!

Travelling provides us with a sense of perspective that is hard to gain in our daily lives. It can remind us that our problems and concerns are often small in the grand scheme of things. When we see how other people live, we may gain a better understanding of what is truly important in life. This newfound perspective can help us let go of the little things that cause us stress and anxiety and focus on the things that truly matter.

It can be a powerful tool for personal growth and reflection. It can teach us about the fragility and beauty of life, the importance of making the most of our time, and the value of different perspectives. So, if you have the opportunity to travel, take it. You may be surprised at how much you learn about yourself and the world around you.

Some people lose out on so many adventures or life changing experiences because they are scared of flying or refuse to travel long haul. Well, don't be scared of flying, just as long as 6 million individual parts stay intact and work together whilst travelling at 500 miles per hour in minus 60 degrees over 6 miles above land whilst relying on the absence of human error and bad weather… you'll be fine! Don't worry about it.

Travelling is not only a way to broaden our horizons, but also to remind us of the preciousness of life and the inevitability of death. Travelling allows us to step out of our comfort zones and immerse ourselves in unfamiliar environments. We are challenged to adapt to new customs, languages, and ways of life, broadening our perspectives and understanding of the world. It can also be an opportunity for self-discovery and personal growth as we confront new challenges and push ourselves beyond our limits.

In many cultures, death is not viewed as something to be feared or avoided but rather as a natural part of the cycle of life. By confronting our mortality through the lens of different cultures, we can gain a new appreciation for the present moment and the opportunities we have to make the most of our time.

Of course, not everyone has the means or the opportunity to travel, but the lesson remains the same: we should strive to live our lives fully and appreciate every moment we have. We should challenge ourselves to step out of our comfort zones, try new things, and broaden our perspectives. By doing so, we can make the most of our time on this earth and live with a sense of purpose and meaning.

Death is a universal phenomenon that is intrinsic to human existence. It is an inevitable and inescapable reality that every living being will eventually encounter. Despite its inevitability, death is a concept that is often avoided, feared, and shrouded in mystery. However, it is a topic that is worth exploring, as it is an integral part of life and can teach us important lessons about the nature of existence.

The first thing to consider when exploring death is its definition. Death is generally defined as the cessation of life or the permanent end of all biological functions that sustain a living organism. From a philosophical perspective, death can be seen as a transition from one state of being to another, or as a passage from the physical to the metaphysical realm.

Death can be a difficult concept to come to terms with, particularly because it involves the loss of life and the inevitable separation from loved ones. The idea of death can also evoke feelings of anxiety, sadness, and fear, as it is an unknown and unpredictable event. However, it is important to remember that death is a natural part of life and that every living being will eventually experience it.

One of the most significant aspects of death is its impact on the living. When someone dies, it can cause profound emotional and psychological effects on those left behind.

Grief, loss and sadness are common reactions to death and can manifest in a variety of ways. It is important to allow ourselves to experience these emotions and to seek support from others, as it can help us to process our feelings and come to terms with the loss.

Death can also be a powerful teacher, as it reminds us of the impermanence and fragility of life. It can inspire us to live more fully and to appreciate the present moment, as we are reminded that life is short and precious. In this sense, death can be seen as a motivator for personal growth and development, as it encourages us to focus on what is truly important in life.

Did I tell you the story about my ex-girlfriend who nearly died? It didn't come up... well, my ex-girlfriend nearly died as she needed blood urgently. Now, I know I may not look like I have a soul but I stepped up and gave her my blood. To cut a long story short, she survived but the relationship didn't. Apparently I make too many innuendos, she asked me to stop so I said I would think long and hard about it... I think that was the final straw. Anyway, after we broke up she requested back my games console and the watch she bought me as presents during our relationship. I know, unbelievable right. Well, I said fine, if you're going to be like that then I want my fucking blood back! You know what she did next, well buckle up, she took her tampon out and threw it at me, then said she will pay me monthly… Apart from that, she's a lovely girl.

From a spiritual perspective, death can be seen as a gateway to another realm or dimension. Many religious and spiritual traditions believe in an afterlife or reincarnation, which can provide comfort and solace to those who have lost a loved one. Others may see it as a new beginning or a transition to another form of existence. The concept of death has long been a source of contemplation and inspiration for philosophers and poets. Many see death as an opportunity for reflection and self-awareness, a reminder that life is fleeting and should be cherished. Some believe that death gives life its meaning and purpose, as it forces us to appreciate the time we have and make the most of it. For others, death is a source of fear and anxiety, an unknown and unpredictable force that cannot be controlled.

Cultures and religions have different beliefs and attitudes toward death. In some cultures, death is seen as a natural and peaceful part of life, and dying is embraced as a natural process. In others, death is viewed as a tragedy and a cause for mourning and grief. Some cultures believe in an afterlife, where the soul or spirit continues to exist after death, while others believe in reincarnation or a cycle of birth and rebirth.

In many religions, death is seen as a transition to another form of existence. In Christianity, for example, death is viewed as a passage to eternal life, where the soul is reunited with God. In Hinduism, death is seen as a continuation of the cycle of birth and rebirth, where the soul is reincarnated into another body. In Buddhism, death is viewed as a natural part of life, and the goal is to achieve enlightenment and liberation from the cycle of rebirth.

Despite the many different views and beliefs about death, it remains a universal experience that we all must face. Well when I die, I have two requests:
One, I want my remains to be scattered around a theme park.
Two, I don't want to be cremated…

In conclusion, death is a complex and multifaceted concept that has fascinated and inspired people for centuries. It is a natural and inevitable part of life that can be viewed in many different ways, depending on culture, religion, and personal beliefs. It is a topic that has fascinated philosophers, poets and scientists for centuries. Whether we see it as an end, a beginning, or a transition, death reminds us of the fragility and preciousness of life. It is a reminder that we should cherish every moment and make the most of the time we have.

The idea of our own mortality can be terrifying, but it is also what gives life its meaning and value. Some believe we are reborn as a different animal. Well, I'd like to come back as a goat, so I can just eat all the time and headbutt anyone who fucking annoys me. Or maybe as a cat, so I can just sleep all day, demand food when needed, cause chaos and knock things over for no fucking reason. But as we're on the topic of travel, maybe I'd prefer to come back as a bird to just eat, travel and shit on things I don't like. Sounds good!

Benefits of travel for personal growth and development

Travelling is not only a fun and exciting activity, but also one that can have a profound impact on personal growth and development. Whether you are exploring a new city or immersing yourself in a foreign culture, travel provides a unique opportunity to learn about yourself and the world around you.

Let's explore some of the benefits of travel for personal growth and development. One of the most significant benefits of travel is the opportunity to step outside of your comfort zone. When you travel, you are often faced with new and unfamiliar situations, which can be both exciting and challenging.

Whether it's navigating unfamiliar streets, communicating in a foreign language or trying out new foods, travel forces you to adapt and learn new skills. Speaking of food, what's the deal with bacon when you go abroad?!? It just isn't the fucking same is it. There's more fat, less pig and it just tastes like it hasn't been cooked with the full intention of causing me some serious health issues. That's what I'm paying for. If you're not going to have proper bacon guys, just don't fucking bother!

Anyway, travelling can build confidence, resilience and help you to develop a more open-minded and flexible approach to life. Travel can also provide valuable perspective on your own life and culture. When you are immersed in a different environment, you can see things from a new and different perspective.

You may realise that some of your assumptions or beliefs are not universal, or that there are alternative ways of living and being. This can broaden your horizons and challenge your assumptions, helping you to develop greater empathy and understanding for people from different backgrounds.

Another benefit of travel is the opportunity to connect with people from different cultures and backgrounds. Whether it's chatting with locals, meeting other travellers, or volunteering in a community, travel can provide valuable opportunities to build meaningful relationships and learn from others. This can expand your social network and expose you to new ideas and perspectives, fostering personal growth and development.

Travel can also provide a break from the routine and stresses of everyday life. Taking time away from work or other responsibilities to explore a new place can be refreshing and rejuvenating.

Did you know that a day on Venus lasts 5,832 hours? Which is the same as a working week on fucking Earth! Whereas the weekend feels like a 30-minute lunch break. You know sometimes I feel like I need a 6 month holiday, twice a fucking year. The trouble is, once upon a time, two careless and reckless people had unprotected sex and now you have to go to fucking work. Splendid!

Well, travelling can help to reduce stress and anxiety and provide a new perspective on what is truly important in life. In addition to these benefits, travel can also be a fun and memorable experience that creates lasting memories and enriches your life. Whether it's hiking in the mountains, exploring a new city, or relaxing on a tropical beach, travel can provide a sense of adventure and excitement that can help you to feel more alive and engaged in the world.

It can be an incredibly rewarding experience that can promote personal growth and development in a variety of ways. From stepping outside of your comfort zone to gaining new perspectives, building relationships, and taking a break from the routine, travel can help you to become a more well-rounded and fulfilled person. But it is not just a way to explore new places and cultures, it can also be an enriching experience that fosters personal growth and development.

The benefits of travel go far beyond just taking a break from our daily routine; they can be both physical and emotional. One of the primary benefits of travel is that it helps us to step out of our comfort zones. When we travel, we are exposed to new environments, cultures, languages, and customs, which can challenge our preconceptions and broaden our perspectives. This can help us to become more adaptable and resilient as we learn to navigate unfamiliar territory.

However, I do seem to have an issue when I go to a place with a warmer climate and it's not just the sun trying to kill me, it's the wasps! They think my head is a fucking flower. They always go for me. In fact, they love gingers. I'm pretty sure their only purpose in life is to eliminate the ginger race. They are vicious little fucks who love an unprovoked attack like they are playing among us. You scale these fuckers up and they look like something out of an alien movie. Yes, I flap. Yes, I scream. And yes, I run away like a little fucking ginger girl. Let's move on.

Anyway, travel can also help us to develop important life skills. For example, travelling can teach us how to problem-solve, communicate effectively with people from different backgrounds, and build self-confidence. These skills are not only useful while travelling but they can also be applied to our daily lives, including our careers and relationships.

It can also be a source of inspiration and creativity. Exposure to new experiences, people, and cultures can ignite our imagination and spark new ideas. Whether it is trying new foods, learning a new language, or simply observing the beauty of a new landscape, travel can inspire us to see the world in new ways and stimulate our creativity.

Travelling can also have a positive impact on our mental and physical health. Studies have shown that travel can reduce stress levels, improve cognitive function, and increase happiness. By stepping outside of our routines and experiencing new environments, we can reduce feelings of burnout and promote overall well-being.

Another way that travel can promote personal growth and development is by exposing us to new perspectives and ideas. When we travel, we are exposed to different cultures, lifestyles, and ways of thinking that we may not have been aware of before. This can help us challenge our own beliefs and expand our understanding of the world. For example, travelling to a country with a vastly different political system or religious beliefs can give us a greater appreciation for the diversity of the human experience. It can also help us understand how different values and beliefs shape society, and how they can lead to different outcomes.

71

By visualising yourself achieving your goal, you can build confidence and focus, which can help you stay on track and achieve success. Embracing uncertainty and overcoming fear in life, there are few things more certain than uncertainty. Despite this, many of us live our lives with a constant fear of the unknown, preferring to stick to what we know and avoid taking risks. However, embracing uncertainty and facing our fears head-on can lead to incredible personal growth and a newfound sense of freedom.

The fear of uncertainty can manifest in many ways, from anxiety about the future to a reluctance to try new things. This fear can be paralysing and prevent us from pursuing our dreams and reaching our full potential. However, when we embrace uncertainty, we open ourselves up to new experiences, opportunities, and perspectives.

One of the keys to embracing uncertainty is learning to let go of control. We may think we have control over our lives, but in reality, there are countless factors outside of our control. Learning to accept this and focus on the things we can control, such as our thoughts, behaviours, and reactions, can help us navigate uncertainty with greater ease. There are some people out there that think life is like a walk in the park.

Well I don't know what park they're walking through because sometimes it feels like mine is jurassic fucking park!

So, instead of viewing uncertainty as a threat, we can choose to see it as an opportunity for growth and learning. This means adopting a mindset of curiosity, openness, and resilience, and being willing to adapt to new situations and challenges. Of course, embracing uncertainty is not always easy, and it often requires facing our fears head- on. However, by taking small steps outside of our comfort zones, we can gradually build up our confidence and resilience, and learn to embrace uncertainty with greater ease.

When we travel, we are often faced with new and unfamiliar situations, from navigating unfamiliar streets to trying new foods and meeting new people. While this can be intimidating, it can also be incredibly rewarding, helping us build confidence, resilience, and a sense of adventure.

By learning to let go of control, adopting a growth mindset, and taking small steps outside of our comfort zones, we can learn to embrace uncertainty with greater ease and live more fulfilling lives. Fear and uncertainty are inevitable parts of life, but they don't have to control us or hold us back from achieving our goals and dreams.

Overcoming fear is another important part of embracing uncertainty. Fear can be paralysing and keep us from taking risks or pursuing our dreams. However, by acknowledging our fears and facing them head-on, we can learn to move past them and take action despite them. One way to overcome fear is through visualisation and positive self-talk. We can visualise ourselves successfully navigating a situation that scares us and use positive self-talk to build confidence in our abilities.

It's also important to remember that failure is not a reflection of our worth or abilities. Failure can be a valuable learning experience that helps us grow and improve. By reframing our perspective on failure and viewing it as a necessary part of the learning process, we can overcome the fear of failure and take more risks.

Life is full of uncertainties, and it is natural to feel anxious and fearful about what the future holds. However, living in a constant state of fear and anxiety can prevent us from experiencing life to its fullest potential. The first step to embracing uncertainty is acknowledging that uncertainty is a natural part of life. No matter how much we plan or prepare, life is unpredictable and full of surprises. When we accept this reality, we can learn to let go of our need for control and embrace the unknown. One way to overcome fear is to face it head-on. Often, the things we fear the most are the things that hold us back from living the life we want. By confronting our fears, we can start to understand them and work towards overcoming them.

In conclusion, embracing uncertainty and overcoming fear can be challenging, but it is essential for personal growth and development. By acknowledging the inevitability of uncertainty, confronting our fears, practising mindfulness, cultivating a positive mindset, and building a support network, we can learn to embrace the unknown and live our lives to the fullest potential.

So, as the title of this book says, you're probably having a bad day... Overworked, underpaid and you probably regret becoming an adult. Well, let me try and cheer you up. One day you will die! That probably didn't help, let me try something else. A few years ago I was drinking too much, eating too much, I wasn't one for the preservation of money, and no one liked me... All of those things are still true. But the major difference is now I just don't give a fuck! The moral of this story is life is 10% what happens to you, and 90% how you react... So, grab yourself a drink and book that fucking holiday!

Techniques for dealing with difficult people

There probably used to be a time when you were so nice, so sweet and so polite. But now you are like fuck you, fuck this and fuck everybody! Well, conflict is an inevitable part of life, and dealing with difficult people can be one of the most challenging situations we encounter. However, there are effective techniques for conflict resolution that can help us manage these situations with more ease and less stress.

You may find that a successful day nowadays is going the whole day without throwing a fucking chair at someone! One technique for dealing with difficult people is to practise active listening. Active listening and effective communication are two skills that can help improve relationships and enhance our personal and professional life.

While it may seem easy to listen and to communicate effectively, it requires intentional effort and practice. Active listening means fully concentrating on what someone is saying, paying attention to their body language, tone, and context to truly understand their message. It involves giving the speaker your full attention, avoiding distractions, and providing feedback to demonstrate that you have understood what they said.

Effective communication involves conveying your message, accurately, and in a way that can be understood by the listener. It also involves listening actively to the other person's message, using appropriate language and tone and being respectful and empathetic in your communication. Improving your active listening and communication skills can enhance your personal and professional relationships, reduce misunderstandings, and improve teamwork and collaboration.

Some strategies to improve your communication skills include:

1. Practise active listening.
When someone is speaking, focus on their words and avoid distractions. Ask clarifying questions and provide feedback to ensure you have understood their message.

2. Use appropriate body language.
Nonverbal cues such as eye contact, posture, and facial expressions can convey important information and demonstrate that you are engaged in the conversation.

3. Speak clearly and concisely.
Use clear and simple language, avoid jargon or technical terms, and speak at an appropriate pace.

4. Be respectful.

Show respect and empathy towards others, and avoid interrupting or dismissing their ideas.

5. Use appropriate tone and volume.

Use a friendly and positive tone, and adjust your volume to suit the situation.

By practising these strategies and being intentional in your communication, you can improve your relationships, reduce misunderstandings, and build a more positive and collaborative environment. To become an active listener, start by eliminating distractions and giving the speaker your full attention. Focus on what they are saying, without interrupting or interjecting with your thoughts. Show that you are engaged by nodding, making eye contact, and using nonverbal cues to indicate that you are following the conversation.

Additionally, effective communication requires not only active listening but also the ability to express oneself clearly and respectfully. To communicate effectively, use "I" statements to express how you feel, avoid blaming or accusing language, and speak clearly and confidently. This means focusing on what the person is saying and trying to understand their perspective without interrupting or judging them. When we listen actively, we can better understand their point of view, and this can help us to find common ground and resolve conflicts more effectively. We can acknowledge their feelings and try to empathise with them, even if we don't agree with their behaviour or actions.

It is important to set boundaries and be clear about what we will and will not tolerate. This can help to prevent further conflict and establish healthy communication in our relationships. We all encounter difficult people in our lives, whether it's a family member, a co-worker, or a stranger. These interactions can be stressful and even escalate to conflicts if not handled properly. Learning conflict resolution techniques can help us manage these difficult situations and maintain positive relationships.

One effective conflict resolution technique is to approach the situation with empathy and understanding. Try to put yourself in the other person's shoes and understand their perspective. Listen actively to what they are saying and validate their feelings. This can help de-escalate the situation and show that you are willing to work towards a resolution.

Another important technique is to avoid attacking the person and instead focus on the issue at hand. Stick to the facts and avoid making assumptions or accusations. Use "I" statements to express how you feel about the situation rather than pointing fingers and blaming the other person.

It's also helpful to explore potential solutions together. Brainstorm ideas and be open to compromise. Look for common ground and try to find a solution that works for everyone involved. This can help build trust and strengthen the relationship. By using these conflict resolution techniques, we can learn to handle difficult people and situations positively and productively. We can also cultivate stronger and healthier relationships with those around us. When dealing with difficult people, it's important to have a plan in place for resolving conflicts.

Here are some techniques that can help:

1. Stay calm and composed.
This can be difficult when someone is getting under your skin, but it's important to keep a level head. Take deep breaths and try to remain calm, even if the other person is being confrontational.

2. Listen actively.
When someone is upset, it's important to let them express their feelings. Listen actively and try to understand their

perspective. You don't have to agree with them, but showing empathy can go a long way in diffusing a tense situation.

3. Use "I" statements.
When expressing your concerns or frustrations, use "I" statements instead of "you" statements. This can help prevent the other person from feeling attacked or defensive.

4. Seek common ground.
Try to find areas of agreement and build on them. This can help shift the focus from the areas of conflict to the areas of agreement.

5. Offer solutions.
Instead of dwelling on the problem, focus on finding solutions. Brainstorm together and come up with a plan that addresses everyone's needs.

6. Be willing to compromise.
Compromise is key when it comes to conflict resolution. Be open to finding a solution that meets everyone's needs, even if it means giving up something you want.

By following these techniques, you can effectively navigate conflicts with difficult people and promote positive relationships with those around you.

You see, a lot of people ask me "Ginge, how do you deal with the haters in life? How do you deal with the people who don't like what you're doing?" Well, surprisingly I actually get a lot of love which is strange, seeing as I'm fucking ginger. However, that doesn't mean I haven't had my fair share of negative comments over the years and the way I deal with them is simply by focusing on the positive ones. If there's a hundred comments and 99 are showing love then I will only focus on them as that means I must be doing something right. There are people out there that will only focus on that one negative comment out of a hundred and it will ruin their day. The key is to be the other way around, you'll be a lot fucking happier.

Keeping a small circle

There's probably two reasons why you don't trust people. One, you don't know them and two, you know them. Well, building a strong support network of friends and family is an essential part of our emotional and mental well-being. We all go through difficult times and face challenges that can be overwhelming. Having a supportive community of people around us can make a world of difference in how we handle these situations.

Firstly, it is important to identify the people in your life who are supportive and reliable. These could be friends, family members, colleagues, or even acquaintances who have demonstrated kindness and understanding toward you in the past. Once you have identified these individuals, it's important to nurture these relationships and build on them.

One way to do this is by being open and honest with your loved ones about how you are feeling. Sharing your struggles and vulnerabilities can be difficult, but it can also be incredibly liberating. It helps to build trust and understanding which can deepen your connections with others. It is important to remember that everyone goes through difficult times and your loved ones may have also faced similar struggles.

Another important aspect of building a support network is being available and present for others. Relationships are a two-way street, and it is important to be there for your loved ones in their times of need as well. Remember, love is like a fart so if you have to force it it's probably shit. So, this can be as simple as lending a listening ear or offering practical support when needed. More so, it is important to remember that building a support network takes time and effort. It is a continuous process that requires regular communication and nurturing.

It is also important to be open to new relationships and connections, as we never know who we may meet that can become an important part of our support system. In addition, building a strong support network is essential for our emotional and mental well-being. It provides us with a sense of belonging, safety, and comfort during difficult times.

By identifying supportive individuals, being open and honest with them and being available for others, we can cultivate meaningful relationships that help us navigate the ups and downs of life. A strong support network can provide emotional support, practical advice, and a sense of belonging.

Here are some tips for building a strong support network:

1. Be open and honest.
Being vulnerable can be scary, but it is important to be open and honest with the people in your life. Let them know how you are feeling and what you are going through.

2. Prioritise relationships.
Make an effort to spend time with the people in your life. This could mean scheduling regular phone calls, having dinner together, or going on a walk.

3. Join groups or clubs.
Joining a group or club that aligns with your interests is a great way to meet new people and build relationships.

4. Use technology.
Social media and other technology can be great tools for staying in touch with people who live far away.

5. Seek out professional help.
In some cases, building a support network of friends and family may not be enough. If you are struggling with mental health issues, it is important to seek out professional help.

Having people in your life who care about you and support you can make all the difference in managing stress and anxiety. When life throws challenges our way, having a group of people we can rely on for emotional support can make all the difference. However, building such a network is not always easy. One of the first steps in building a support network is identifying the people in our lives who we can turn to when we need help. This may include family members, friends, colleagues, or even acquaintances. It is important to choose people who we trust and who we feel comfortable opening up to.

We need to be able to communicate effectively with the people in our network to receive the support we need. This means being open and honest about our feelings and needs, as well as actively listening to the perspectives and experiences of others. In addition to communication, it is important to establish boundaries within our support network. We need to be clear about what kind of support we need and what kind of support we can offer in return. This can help prevent any misunderstandings or resentment that may arise if expectations are not clear.

We need to make time for the people in our network and show them that we value their presence in our lives. This can include regular phone calls, coffee dates, or even simple messages of appreciation. In conclusion, building a support network of friends and family is crucial for maintaining good mental health. By identifying the people we can trust, communicating effectively, establishing boundaries, and putting in the effort to maintain our relationships, we can create a strong foundation of support that can help us through life's challenges.

Empathy is a critical component of healthy relationships. It involves the ability to understand and share the feelings of another person. People who I don't have empathy for are people who smack their lips when eating... Jesus Christ. What the actual fuck! Where did these people grow up? A fucking forest! These animals need to be sectioned or as a minimum when they commit this atrocious crime it should at least affect their credit rating. It's not hard. Going to space is hard. Holding down many jobs to provide for your kids as a single parent is hard. Keeping your dick flaccid when a stunning masseuse massages you and her hands go up your thighs is hard. But, closing your mouth when you chew is not fucking hard. Sort your fucking life out.

Anyway, when we empathise with others we can connect on a deeper level, build trust, and foster intimacy. However, empathy is not always a natural skill, and it requires practice to develop. One way to cultivate empathy is through empathy exercises. These exercises can help us become more aware of our emotions and the emotions of others, which can lead to more meaningful and fulfilling relationships. Here are some empathy exercises to try:

1. Mirror Emotions.

This exercise involves mirroring the emotions of another person. If someone is happy, you should try to reflect that happiness. If someone is sad, try to reflect that sadness. By mirroring their emotions, you are demonstrating that you understand and are in tune with their feelings.

2. Active Listening.

Active listening involves paying attention to what someone is saying without interrupting or judging. It also involves asking questions to gain a better understanding of the person's perspective. When you actively listen to someone, you show that you care about what they have to say and that you are interested in understanding their point of view.

3. Role-Playing.

Role-playing involves putting yourself in someone else's shoes to better understand their perspective. It can be helpful in situations where there is conflict or misunderstanding. By role-playing, you can gain a better understanding of the other person's point of view and work towards a resolution.

4. Practising Gratitude.

Practising gratitude involves reflecting on the positive aspects of your life and expressing gratitude for them. It can help you become more empathetic by fostering a sense of appreciation for the things you have and the people in your life. When you are grateful, you are more likely to recognise the value of others and the importance of their feelings.

5. Sharing Experiences.

Sharing experiences involves opening up about your own emotions and experiences. It can help others feel more comfortable sharing their feelings and can create a deeper sense of connection. By sharing your experiences, you also demonstrate that you understand and empathise with the emotions of others.

Empathy is an essential component of healthy relationships, and empathy exercises can help us develop and cultivate this critical skill. By practising active listening, role-playing, and expressing gratitude, we can become more aware of our emotions and the emotions of others, leading to more meaningful and fulfilling relationships.

Ultimately, it's important to practise self-empathy as well. This means treating yourself with kindness and understanding and acknowledging your feelings and needs. By being more empathetic towards yourself, you can develop greater empathy towards others as well. Empathy is an important skill that can help us build meaningful relationships and connect with those around us.

By practising empathy exercises like actively listening, doing kind deeds for others, practising self-empathy and putting yourself in someone else's shoes, you can cultivate greater empathy and become a more compassionate and understanding person. I wouldn't always advise walking a mile in my ginger shoes though, you'll end up at the fucking pub.

By practising empathy exercises regularly, we can improve our ability to connect with others and build meaningful relationships. This can lead to greater happiness and fulfilment in our personal and professional lives.

Coping methods to deal with anxiety and depression

There are five things you can quit right now:

1. Trying to make everyone happy.
2. Thinking you're not good enough.
3. Being scared of failure.
4. Overthinking.
5. Giving a fuck.

In fact, write all your problems down on a piece of paper, make a paper plane out of it and turn them into flying fucks!

We live in a world that can be oppressive, with demands and stressors coming at us from all angles. Whether it's work, school, relationships, or the constant barrage of news and information, it's easy to feel like we're constantly on edge.

Anxiety and depression are two of the most common mental health conditions affecting millions of people worldwide. They can be caused by various factors, including genetics, life events and chemical imbalances in the brain. When anxiety and depression starts to take over, it's essential to prioritise our well-being and practice self-care. Self-care is not a luxury, but a necessity for managing and promoting our mental health. So in this part, we'll explore some self-care tips that can help you manage and prioritise your well-being so you can live a more fulfilling life.

From establishing a self-care routine to practising mindfulness and staying connected with loved ones, these tips can help you build resilience and navigate life's challenges with greater ease and grace. So, take a deep breath, and let's dive into some practical self-care strategies that can help you find peace and balance amidst life's chaos. Or as I like to call it, a fucking shitshow.

One of the most important aspects of self-care is establishing a routine that works for you. This can include things like setting aside time each day for exercise, meditation, or relaxation. It can also mean creating boundaries around work or technology use so that you have time to recharge and connect with yourself and others.

Staying connected with friends and family is also an important part of self-care. When we feel supported and connected to others, we're better able to cope and build resilience. When we prioritise our relationships and invest in our social networks, we're more likely to feel a sense of belonging and purpose. Talking to a trusted friend or family member can provide a sense of comfort and understanding whilst support groups can provide a safe and welcoming environment for individuals to share their experiences and connect with others who are going through similar struggles.

Taking care of our physical health is an essential aspect of self-care. This can include things like eating a healthy diet, getting enough sleep and engaging in regular exercise or movement. I joke about drinking and eating badly but it's true, when we take care of our bodies, we're better able to manage stress and feel more energised and resilient. So, take some time for yourself today and remember that self-care is not selfish, but an essential part of living a happy, healthy life.

Coping with anxiety and depression can be challenging, but many methods can help individuals manage their symptoms and improve their overall well-being like self-care practices such as exercise, meditation, and mindfulness.

Engaging in hobbies or activities that bring joy can also be an effective coping mechanism. This can include reading, writing, listening to music, or participating in sports or other physical activities. Individuals need to identify what activities bring them joy and make time for them regularly.

Anxiety and depression are two of the most common mental health issues that people face. According to the World Health Organization (WHO), more than 264 million people globally suffer from depression, and around 284 million have anxiety disorders. Coping with these conditions can be challenging, but it is possible.

One of the most effective coping methods is therapy. Therapy provides individuals with the tools and skills they need to manage their emotions and develop healthier thought patterns. Cognitive-behavioural therapy (CBT), for example, is a type of therapy that focuses on changing negative thought patterns and behaviours that contribute to anxiety and depression. Other types of therapy, such as psychodynamic therapy and interpersonal therapy, can also be effective. It is essential to find a therapist who is a good fit, someone who understands your condition and can help you work through it. Therapy can be expensive, but there are many resources available for individuals who cannot afford it.

Meditation involves focusing your attention on your breath, a sound, or an object, and allowing your thoughts to come and go without attaching to them. Studies have shown that mindfulness and meditation can help reduce symptoms of anxiety and depression. There are several apps available which can help you with meditation.

Exercise is also an excellent coping method for anxiety and depression. Exercise releases endorphins, which are feel-good chemicals that boost mood and reduce stress. Engaging in physical activity can also improve sleep, increase energy levels, and boost self-esteem. It is recommended to aim for at least 30-minutes of physical activity per day. Diet is another essential factor in coping with anxiety and depression. Eating a healthy, balanced diet can help regulate mood and reduce symptoms. Getting enough sleep is also important for managing anxiety and depression, as lack of sleep can exacerbate symptoms.

Social support is crucial for coping with anxiety and depression. Talking to friends and family about your feelings can help reduce the sense of isolation and provide comfort. Joining a support group or engaging in community activities can also provide a sense of belonging and support.

It is important to remember that everyone copes differently, and there is no one-size-fits-all solution. It may take time and effort to find the right coping methods, but it is possible to manage these conditions effectively and lead a fulfilling life. Coping with anxiety and depression can be challenging, but many coping methods can help individuals manage their symptoms and improve their quality of life.

Signs and triggers for anxiety and depression

Anxiety and depression are two mental health conditions that can have a significant impact on a person's daily life. These conditions can be triggered by a wide range of factors, such as stress, trauma, and genetics. Identifying triggers and warning signs can help individuals better manage their anxiety and depression and seek professional help if necessary.

One of the first steps in identifying triggers and warning signs is to become more aware of one's thoughts and feelings. Often, people with anxiety and depression may not recognise the early signs of their conditions, making it difficult to manage them before they escalate. It's important to take note of the events or situations that tend to trigger anxiety or depression. For example, if a person experiences high levels of stress at work or school, they may find that their anxiety or depression symptoms worsen during those times. Additionally, certain social situations, such as parties or large gatherings, may also be triggers for some people.

Another way to identify triggers and warning signs is to pay attention to physical symptoms. Anxiety and depression can manifest physically in various ways, such as headaches, muscle tension, and fatigue. By noticing when these symptoms occur and what events or situations precede them, individuals can gain insight into what triggers their anxiety or depression. Once triggers have been identified, individuals can work to develop coping strategies to manage their anxiety and depression.

If an individual's anxiety or depression symptoms become unmanageable, it's important to seek professional help. Mental health professionals can guide on coping strategies, medication management, and therapy options to help individuals manage their conditions. By becoming more self-aware and seeking professional help when necessary, individuals can take control of their mental health and lead a more fulfilling life.

Triggers are specific situations, events, or people that can cause a person to experience symptoms of anxiety or depression. Warning signs are physical, emotional, or behavioural changes that indicate a person may be at risk for a more severe episode of anxiety or depression. Common triggers for anxiety and depression include stressful life events such as job loss, financial difficulties, or the death of a loved one. Chronic stress from work or relationships can also contribute to the development of anxiety and depression.

Social isolation and loneliness can also be triggers for anxiety and depression, especially for individuals who struggle with social anxiety. Warning signs of anxiety and depression can vary depending on the individual, but may include changes in mood or behaviour, difficulty sleeping, increased or decreased appetite, loss of interest in activities, feelings of hopelessness or helplessness, and thoughts of self-harm or suicide. It is important to recognise these warning signs and seek help from a mental health professional or support system before the symptoms become severe.

One effective way to identify triggers and warning signs is to keep a journal or log of your symptoms. This can help you to identify patterns and triggers that may be contributing to your anxiety or depression. It can also help you to recognise warning signs before a more severe episode occurs. Once you have identified your triggers and warning signs, you can take steps to manage and prevent them.

This may include practising relaxation techniques such as deep breathing or meditation, engaging in regular exercise or physical activity, seeking social support from friends and family, and seeking professional help from a mental health provider. It is important to remember that anxiety and depression are treatable conditions, and with proper treatment and support, individuals can learn to manage their symptoms and improve their quality of life.

Warning signs of anxiety can include excessive worrying, irritability, restlessness, difficulty concentrating, muscle tension, and sleep disturbances. Depression warning signs may include feelings of sadness, hopelessness, fatigue, loss of interest in activities, changes in appetite or weight, and difficulty sleeping. It is important to note that these warning signs may vary in severity and duration. Some individuals may experience occasional mild symptoms, while others may experience more severe and persistent symptoms. If you notice these warning signs in yourself or someone else, it is essential to seek help from a mental health professional.

Overall, recognising triggers and warning signs of anxiety and depression is essential for maintaining good mental health. Seeking professional help and practising self-care can help individuals effectively manage symptoms and improve their overall well-being.

Self-care practices for anxiety and depression

Anxiety and depression can be challenging to manage, but incorporating self-care practices into your routine can help alleviate symptoms and promote overall well-being. Self-care is about taking care of yourself mentally, emotionally, and physically. It's essential to recognise that self-care is not a one-size-fits-all solution, and what works for one person may not work for another. Therefore, it's crucial to experiment with different self-care practices to see what resonates with you.

Here are some self-care practices for managing anxiety and depression:

1. Prioritise sleep.
Getting enough sleep is crucial for managing anxiety and depression. Aim for 7-8 hours of sleep per night and establish a consistent sleep routine. Consider using a sleep app or diffusing a lavender essential oil to help promote relaxation.

2. Practice mindfulness meditation.
Mindfulness meditation can help calm the mind and reduce anxiety and depression symptoms. Take 10-15 minutes each day to practise mindfulness meditation.

3. Engage in physical activity.

Regular exercise has been shown to reduce anxiety and depression symptoms. Find an activity that you enjoy and aim for at least 30 minutes of exercise per day. It could be as simple as going for a walk, practising yoga, or lifting weights.

4. Connect with others.

Social support is crucial for managing anxiety and depression. Spend time with friends and family, join a support group, or connect with others online. It's essential to have people you can turn to for support and encouragement.

5. Practice self-compassion.

Be kind and compassionate with yourself. It's okay to have bad days or make mistakes. Practice self-talk that is positive and encouraging.

6. Eat a healthy diet.

Eating a diet rich in fruits, vegetables, whole grains, and lean protein can help boost your mood and energy levels. Limit your intake of processed and sugary foods, which can lead to mood swings and energy crashes.

7. Engage in hobbies and activities you enjoy.

Engaging in activities you enjoy can help reduce stress and

anxiety. Take up a new hobby, read a book, or watch a movie. Make time for things that make you happy.

8. Take Breaks.

It is essential to take breaks from work or other stressful situations to give yourself time to relax and recharge. Try to schedule regular breaks throughout the day, even if they are just a few minutes.

Managing anxiety and depression requires a multifaceted approach that includes self-care practices. Incorporating these practices into your daily routine can help you feel better mentally, emotionally, and physically. Remember to be patient with yourself and experiment with different self-care practices to find what works best for you. Self-care practices are crucial for maintaining good mental health and managing anxiety and depression.

Some practices that work for one person may not be effective for another. Experimenting with different self-care practices and finding what works best can take time, but it is important to prioritise self-care and It is important to seek help if symptoms of anxiety or depression are interfering with daily life or causing significant distress.

Mindfulness and meditation techniques can be incredibly powerful tools for regulating your emotions and helping to manage anxiety and depression. Mindfulness can also be the practice of being present and fully engaged in the current moment, without judgement or distraction. Meditation is a specific technique used to cultivate mindfulness. There are many different types of meditation, but they all share the goal of training the mind to focus on the present moment.

Some popular types of meditation include:

1. Mindfulness meditation.
This type of meditation involves paying attention to your breath and body sensations and observing your thoughts and emotions without judgement.

2. Loving-kindness meditation.
Also known as "metta" meditation, this technique involves cultivating feelings of love, compassion, and kindness towards yourself and others.

3. Body scan meditation.
This technique involves bringing your attention to different parts of your body, noticing any physical sensations or tension, and practising relaxation.

4. Mantra meditation.

This technique involves repeating a word or phrase to help focus the mind and cultivate a sense of calm and inner peace. Research has shown that regular mindfulness and meditation practice can help to reduce symptoms of anxiety and depression, as well as improve overall emotional well-being.

Here are some mindfulness and meditation techniques that you can try:

1. Deep breathing.

Taking slow, deep breaths can help to calm the nervous system and reduce feelings of anxiety. Try inhaling for a count of four, holding your breath for a count of seven, and exhaling for a count of eight.

2. Body scan.

Lie down or sit comfortably and bring your attention to each part of your body, starting at your toes and working your way up to the top of your head. Notice any physical sensations or tension, and try to release any areas of tightness.

3. Guided meditation.

There are many guided meditation videos and apps available that can help you to cultivate mindfulness and relaxation.

4. Mindful movement.

Practices like yoga, tai chi, and qigong combine movement with breath and mindfulness, making them great options for emotional regulation.

5. Gratitude practice.

Taking time each day to reflect on things that you are grateful for can help to cultivate a sense of positivity and reduce negative thinking patterns.

By incorporating mindfulness and meditation into your daily routine, you can learn to regulate your emotions more effectively and manage anxiety and depression more successfully. Remember to be patient with yourself as you begin this practice, and don't hesitate to seek out additional support if needed. It is important to remember that seeking help is not a sign of weakness or failure, but rather a proactive step towards improving one's mental health and overall well-being.

It is important to have a support system of family and friends who can offer emotional support and encouragement. This can involve talking openly and honestly about struggles and feelings, as well as engaging in positive social activities and hobbies. It takes courage to reach out for support and take steps toward improving one's mental health. Taking care of one's mental health is an ongoing process, and seeking help and support when needed is a vital part of that process

There are many online resources available for those seeking help for anxiety and depression. These resources can include online therapy sessions, self-help tools, and forums where individuals can connect with others and share their experiences. Overall, it's important to remember that seeking professional help for anxiety and depression is a sign of strength, not weakness. By taking care of your mental health, you can improve your overall well-being and quality of life.

So, if you're having a bad day and thinking about giving up, try this. Grab two banknotes of the same value and then crumple one up and leave the other. That crumpled banknote now looks like it has been through the wars, not in great condition, run down and in bad shape. It's safe to say that it's not perfect. However, that note is worth exactly the same as the other note. The moral of this story is no matter what you've been through, no matter what your circumstances are and no matter how worthless you feel, you will never lose your true value. So, don't beat yourself up and think you're not worth it, because you fucking are!

Building a support network

Building a support network of friends and family is an essential part of emotional self-care. Having a group of individuals that you can turn to in times of stress and difficulty can provide you with the strength and resilience necessary to overcome life's challenges.

To build a strong support network, it's important to first identify the people in your life who can serve as sources of emotional support. These individuals should be people who you trust, who are reliable, and who genuinely care about your well-being. It's also important to ensure that your support network is diverse, including people from different backgrounds, perspectives, and experiences.

Once you've identified the people in your life who can serve as sources of emotional support, it's important to nurture those relationships. This means making time for these individuals, actively listening to their needs and concerns, and being there for them in times of need.

Additionally, taking care of yourself physically can help you to better manage difficult emotions and cope with stress.

By prioritising your emotional well-being, you can build resilience and strength that will help you to thrive in all areas of your life.

It is often said that a person is as strong as their support system and this could not be truer when it comes to emotional well-being. A robust support network can help us cope with stress, anxiety, and other mental health issues. It provides us with a sense of belonging, love, and acceptance, which are crucial for our emotional stability.

One of the main benefits of having a support network is that it can help us manage the challenges that life throws at us. When we face a difficult situation, it is easy to feel overwhelmed and helpless. However, having a support network in place can help us feel more capable and confident in our ability to overcome the challenge. Whether it's dealing with a personal crisis, work-related stress, or a family problem, a support network can offer us the guidance and support we need to navigate the situation successfully.

Another benefit of having a support network is that it can help us maintain a positive outlook on life. When we are surrounded by people who love and care for us, we are more likely to have a sense of optimism and hope for the future. This positive mindset can help us overcome obstacles and setbacks, making it easier to bounce back from challenges that might otherwise seem insurmountable. In addition to providing emotional support, a support network can also offer us practical help when we need it. This could include anything from helping us move house to offering us a place to stay if we need it. When we have a support network in place, we know that there are people we can rely on in times of need.

Building a support network of friends and family does require some effort on our part. It means taking the time to build and maintain relationships with people who matter to us. This may involve making regular phone calls, catching up for coffee, or spending time with loved ones regularly. It also means being willing to ask for help when we need it and being open to accepting the support that others offer us.

It's also important to remember that building a support network is not just about receiving support; it's also about giving it. Being there for our friends and family when they need us can be incredibly rewarding, and it helps to strengthen our relationships and build a sense of community. By being there for others, we can also create a sense of purpose and meaning in our own lives. In conclusion, building a support network of friends and family is crucial for our emotional well-being. It provides us with a sense of belonging, love, and acceptance, which are essential for our mental health. By taking the time to build and maintain relationships with those who matter to us, we can ensure that we have the support we need to cope with life's challenges and maintain a positive outlook on life.

Here are some tips for building a strong support network:

1. Reach out to friends and family.
Don't be afraid to reach out to those close to you and let them know you are struggling. It can be hard to ask for help, but it's important to remember that your loved ones care about you and want to be there for you.

2. Join a support group.
Consider joining a support group where you can connect with others who are going through similar experiences. This can provide you with a sense of community and support.

3. Stay in touch.
Make an effort to stay in touch with friends and family, even if it's just a quick text or phone call. Regular communication can help you feel connected and supported.

4. Be open and honest.
When talking to your support network, be open and honest about your feelings and struggles. This can help others

understand what you're going through and provide more meaningful support.

5. Express gratitude.
Let your support network know how much you appreciate their support and how much it means to you. This can help strengthen your relationships and foster a sense of mutual appreciation and support.

Remember, this takes time and effort. With time and persistence, you can build a strong support network that will help you through even the toughest of times. Life can be challenging, but it's important to remember that we are all in this together. With the right mindset, guidance, and support, we can overcome any obstacle and thrive.

Remember that you are not alone, and it's okay to ask for help when needed. Keep pushing forward, and you will get through whatever challenges. Life is a journey that is full of ups and downs, successes and failures, joys, and sorrows. It is important to remember that each experience is an opportunity for growth and learning and that we have the power to choose how we respond to life's challenges.

Coping with grief and loss

Grief and loss are also inevitable parts of the human experience. Whether it's the death of a loved one, the end of a relationship, or a major life change, we all experience loss at some point in our lives.

Coping with grief and loss can be a difficult and painful process, but it's important to learn how to manage these emotions healthily. One of the most important things to remember when dealing with grief and loss is to give yourself time to heal. Everyone grieves in their way and at their own pace, so it's important not to compare your grieving process to others or to feel like you're not handling things well. Allow yourself to feel whatever emotions come up without judgement or criticism. It's also important to take care of yourself during this time.

Try to focus on positive memories and experiences. Take time to reflect on the happy times you shared with the person you have lost or the positive aspects of the relationship that ended. This can help shift your focus away from feelings of loss and sadness and towards feelings of gratitude and appreciation.

However, whether it's the loss of a loved one, a pet, a job, or a relationship, everyone experiences grief and loss in some form or another. Grief can be physically and emotionally exhausting, so it's important to prioritise self-care. Connecting with others who have experienced similar losses can also be helpful. It's also important to give yourself time to grieve. The grieving process is not linear, and it can take weeks, months, or even years to come to terms with a loss. Be patient with yourself and allow yourself to feel your emotions as they arise. Remember that healing takes time and that it's okay to take things one day at a time.

Losing someone we love is a heart-wrenching experience that everyone goes through at some point in their lives. Coping with grief and loss can be a challenging and painful process, and it can take time to come to terms with the loss. It is essential to remember that there is no right or wrong way to grieve. Everyone copes with loss differently, and the process can be complex and unique to each individual.

One of the most crucial aspects of coping with grief and loss is allowing yourself to feel and process your emotions. It is common to experience a range of emotions, including sadness, anger, guilt, and confusion, among others. Suppressing these emotions can be detrimental to your well-being and can lead to more significant problems down the road. Instead, it is essential to let yourself feel and express your emotions in healthy ways. This could mean talking to a trusted friend or family member, seeking professional help, or finding a creative outlet to express your feelings.

It is also important to find ways to honour and remember the person you have lost. This could mean creating a memorial, planting a tree, or doing something they loved in their memory. Finding a way to keep their memory alive can be a healing and comforting way to cope with the loss.

The power of positive thinking

Well, that got serious didn't it. I hope it was somewhat educational, like women in conversation. I love listening to women's conversations, it's educational as fuck, I learn a lot! Last time I listened to a woman's conversation I learnt that women know… they just know. Even if they don't know, they will know. Men might not understand this but women will, because they know. Another thing I learnt was if you don't judge a woman by pounds then she won't judge you by inches. Now that's good to know. Another thing I learnt was that a woman will spend more time wondering what men are thinking about than what men spend actually fucking thinking… interesting. One thing I have always known about women is that they can look after themselves, they can hold their own. In fact, the only time when a woman is helpless is when their nail polish is drying. Other than that you better watch the fuck out!

Anyway, now on to positive thinking. Adversity is an inevitable part of life, it can come in many forms such as financial struggles, relationship issues, health problems, and more. While adversity can be challenging and overwhelming, it is important to remember that we have the power to control our thoughts and our attitudes toward these difficult situations.

The way we think about adversity can greatly impact how we feel and how we respond to the challenges we face. One way to approach adversity is through the power of positive thinking. Positive thinking is the practice of focusing on the good in a situation and approaching challenges with a hopeful outlook. This approach does not mean ignoring the reality of a difficult situation, but rather choosing to see it from a different perspective. The power of positive thinking lies in the fact that our thoughts and beliefs can greatly influence our emotions and actions.

When we approach challenges with a positive mindset, we are more likely to feel hopeful and motivated to take action toward finding solutions. We become more resilient and better equipped to handle adversity. For example, imagine that you have lost your job unexpectedly. This situation can be very stressful and overwhelming, and it is natural to feel worried and anxious. However, instead of focusing on the negative aspects of the situation, you can choose to approach it with a positive mindset. You can focus on the opportunities that this change may bring, such as the chance to pursue a career that you are truly passionate about or to learn new skills that may lead to future success.

One way to cultivate a positive mindset is through gratitude. By focusing on the good in our lives and expressing gratitude for the things we have, we can shift our perspective towards a more positive outlook. This can be as simple as taking time each day to reflect on the things you are grateful for, or writing them down in a gratitude journal.

Another way to develop positive thinking is through affirmations. Affirmations are positive statements that help to reinforce a desired mindset or belief. By repeating affirmations to yourself regularly, you can train your mind to think positively and become more resilient in the face of adversity.

For instance, did you know the average horse weighs 1,050 pounds with an average size penis of 19 and a half inches. That equates to roughly 54 per inch, but the average human male weighs 185 pounds, so in order to be "hung like a horse" you would roughly need a 3 and a half inch penis. The moral of the story is, if you can reach such a length, then you can claim to be "hung like a horse" without it being a fucking seahorse. Positive thinking… You're welcome.

The power of positive thinking can be a valuable tool for overcoming adversity and finding success in life. By focusing on the good in any situation and approaching challenges with a hopeful mindset, we can cultivate resilience and become better equipped to handle whatever life may throw our way. The power of positive thinking can be a powerful tool to help individuals overcome adversity. It is a mindset that focuses on the positive aspects of a situation rather than dwelling on the negative.

Positive thinking is not about denying reality or ignoring challenges, but rather about choosing to approach challenges with a positive attitude. When faced with adversity, it is easy to feel overwhelmed, stressed, and anxious. Negative thoughts and emotions can quickly take over, leading to a downward spiral. However, by focusing on the positive, individuals can change their mindset and approach challenges more constructively and productively.

I know that it's hard. I know that it's easier said than done, especially when it comes to people. Like when people talk loudly on the phone. There are things in life I will never understand: women, how an old nokia phone is so indestructible it could survive a nuclear bomb, and why do people feel the need to shout down the fucking phone! What do you think you're achieving? What do they even have the phone for, it's not needed as they're shouting so loudly even the astronauts on the international fucking space station can here them. These people do it on the train, on the bus, at a restaurant, pub, bar or even in a supermarket. But apparently taking someone's phone off them and throwing it on the floor, then stamping on it 69 times is a crime. I learnt the hard way, but I feel like it was perfectly reasonable.

Or when someone keeps sniffing in public. Blow your fucking noise you absolute germ sperm. It's not actually the germ spreading that annoys me. It's the noise. Noises really get on my ginger fucking nerves. You've tried beating gravity by forcing snot back up your nose making this horrific noise that sounds like a sports car is about to explode. Blow your nose or fuck off!

Or when people call you without prior warning. What are you doing? Where was my advance warning? Fuck off! Yes, I was on my phone. Yes, I was scrolling. And yes, I could have answered very easily, but I will just sit here and wait for you to hang up. Unless it's an emergency i.e. someone on the brink of certain death, I think it's totally unacceptable to call without making a prior official appointment. I've got stuff to do. And by that I mean I will just carry on scrolling through social media once you've stopped trying to ruin my day.

What about when friends or family show up at your house uninvited… Again, what the fuck are you doing? Same as my previous rant… Fuck off! If that was unacceptable then this is damn right inexcusable. I don't care that you're a so-called loved one, I will call the police.

Or when people who aren't ready to order their food. Hurry the fuck up! You knew you were coming here, you had all that time and you've done it hundreds of times, so why the fuck are you taking so long! I don't mean to be overdramatic or anything, but if I say I'm hungry then we've got a matter of minutes before I turn into a completely different fucking person. Just hurry the fuck up!

Anyway, back to positive thinking… Positive thinking can help individuals cope with stress, improve their mood, and increase their resilience. By focusing on the positive aspects of a situation, individuals can find the motivation and energy to keep going even when things get tough. For example, imagine someone who has lost their job. They could dwell on the negative aspects of the situation, such as financial stress and uncertainty about the future. Alternatively, they could choose to focus on the positive aspects, such as the opportunity to explore new career paths and the chance to take a break from the daily grind.

Positive thinking can also have physical benefits, such as improving immune function and reducing the risk of chronic diseases. A positive mindset can lead to healthier behaviours, such as regular exercise and healthy eating, which can further improve physical health.

While it may not always be easy to maintain a positive attitude, there are several strategies individuals can use to cultivate a more positive mindset. These include practising gratitude, engaging in positive self-talk, surrounding oneself with positive influences, and focusing on solutions rather than problems. In conclusion, the power of positive thinking should not be underestimated. By choosing to focus on the positive aspects of a situation, individuals can improve their mood, cope with stress, and increase their resilience. While it may not always be easy, cultivating a positive mindset can have numerous benefits for both mental and physical health. When faced with adversity, it can be easy to succumb to negative thoughts and emotions. However, adopting a positive mindset can make all the difference in overcoming challenges and achieving success.

So, I bumped into a different ex-girlfriend the other week, always awkward. We broke up because apparently I ruined her birthday… Lies, I didn't even know it was her fucking birthday. I'm surprised she broke up with me anyway, she always used to call me her sex machine. I know right, well her actual words were you are a fucking tool but again, I'm trying to focus on the positives.

The power of positive thinking lies in its ability to shift our focus from what we can't control to what we can control. When we focus on positive thoughts and possibilities, we are more likely to take positive actions and find solutions to our problems. Positive thinking also has a profound impact on our emotional and physical well-being. Studies have shown that people who adopt a positive outlook are better equipped to cope with stress, have stronger immune systems, and experience a greater sense of overall well-being.

One effective way to cultivate a positive mindset is through affirmations. Affirmations are positive statements that can help us focus on our strengths and abilities. By repeating these statements regularly, we can reprogram our minds to think positively and believe in ourselves.

Another powerful tool for positive thinking is visualisation. By visualising ourselves succeeding and achieving our goals, we can boost our confidence and motivation. Visualisation can also help us overcome fear and anxiety by allowing us to mentally rehearse how we will handle challenging situations.

Gratitude is another important aspect of positive thinking. When we focus on what we are thankful for, we shift our attention away from our problems and toward the positive aspects of our lives. Gratitude can help us maintain a positive perspective and foster resilience in the face of adversity.

Surrounding ourselves with positive people can have a significant impact on our mindset. When we spend time with people who uplift and inspire us, we are more likely to adopt a positive outlook and find success in our endeavours. The power of positive thinking cannot be overstated. By adopting a positive mindset and focusing on our strengths, we can overcome adversity, achieve our goals, and experience greater happiness and well-being. Strategies for making the most of every moment in life. Life is a precious gift, and every moment we have is an opportunity to make the most of it.

However, we often get caught up in the chaos of life and forget to savour the present moment. It's easy to get caught up in our worries about the future or regrets about the past, but by doing so, we miss out on the beauty and potential of the present. To make the most of every moment in life, we must first learn to be present. This means focusing our attention on what is happening right now, rather than worrying about what might happen in the future or what has happened in the past. Mindfulness meditation is an excellent way to develop this skill. By regularly practising mindfulness, we can train our minds to be fully present and engage with the world around us.

Another way to make the most of every moment in life is to prioritise the things that matter most to us. This means taking the time to reflect on our values and what we want to achieve in life. By identifying what is most important to us, we can focus our energy and resources on those areas that will bring us the most fulfilment and happiness.

Setting goals is an important part of this process. Goals give us direction and purpose and help us to stay focused on what is important. However, it's important to set realistic goals that are aligned with our values and priorities. Setting unrealistic goals can lead to disappointment and frustration, which can detract from our overall sense of well-being.

Making the most of every moment in life requires a combination of mindfulness, goal-setting, gratitude, and self-care. By cultivating these skills and practices, we can develop a more positive and fulfilling outlook on life, and make the most of every moment we have. Living life to the fullest is a common goal for many people. We all want to make the most of every moment and create meaningful experiences that bring us joy and fulfilment. However, with the hustle and bustle of daily life, it can be easy to get caught up in routine and forget to enjoy the little things.

Here are some strategies for making the most of every moment in life:

1. Be present.
One of the most important things you can do to make the most of every moment is to be present. It's easy to get distracted by thoughts about the past or worries about the future, but this can prevent you from fully experiencing and enjoying the present moment. Practice mindfulness and focus on the here and now.

2. Take risks.
Trying new things and taking risks can help you break out of your comfort zone and experience life in a new way. Whether it's trying a new hobby, travelling to a new place, or starting a new job, taking risks can lead to new opportunities and experiences.

3. Practise gratitude.
Cultivating an attitude of gratitude can help you appreciate the little things in life and find joy in everyday experiences. Take time each day to reflect on the things you are grateful for, whether it's a warm cup of coffee, a good conversation with a friend, or a beautiful sunset.

4. Connect with others.

Building strong relationships and connections with others can add richness and meaning to your life. Make time for the people you care about and cultivate new friendships by getting involved in community groups or volunteering.

5. Live in alignment with your values.

When you live in alignment with your values, you are more likely to feel fulfilled and content with your life. Take time to reflect on what is truly important to you and make choices that align with those values.

6. Embrace change.

Change can be scary, but it can also be an opportunity for growth and self-discovery. Rather than resisting change, embrace it and see where it takes you.

7. Practice self-care.

Taking care of yourself is essential for making the most of every moment in life. Prioritise self-care by getting enough sleep, eating well, and engaging in activities that bring you joy and relaxation.

In summary, life is full of opportunities to make the most of every moment. By being present, taking risks, practising gratitude, connecting with others, living in alignment with your values, embracing change, and prioritising self-care, you can create the life you desire.

By implementing some simple strategies, you can make the most of every moment in life and find greater fulfilment and satisfaction in your everyday experiences. One of the most effective strategies for maximising your time and energy is to practise mindfulness. This involves being fully present in the moment, without judgement or distraction, and simply experiencing the world around you as it is. By cultivating a mindful mindset, you can develop a deeper appreciation for the simple pleasures in life and find greater meaning and purpose in each moment.

Take the time to reflect on what truly matters to you, both in the short-term and the long-term, and making a conscious effort to align your actions with your values and aspirations whilst setting clear goals and priorities. Whether you're striving to achieve a specific career milestone, deepen a personal relationship, or simply live more fully in the present moment, having a clear sense of purpose can help you stay focused and motivated even in the face of obstacles and setbacks.

Of course, life is never without its challenges and setbacks, and sometimes it can be difficult to maintain a positive outlook in the face of adversity. However, by cultivating a growth mindset and embracing the lessons that come with failure and disappointment, you can turn even the toughest experiences into opportunities for growth and self-improvement. Rather than dwelling on your shortcomings or setbacks, try to reframe them as learning experiences and opportunities for personal development. So, don't let the chaos and unpredictability of life hold you back, take control of your experiences and make the most of every moment!

Throughout this book, we have explored various topics such as setting goals, overcoming self-doubt, developing a personal brand, balancing work and life, travelling, embracing uncertainty, coping with grief and loss, and managing anxiety and depression.

These topics all touch on different aspects of our lives, but they share a common theme: the importance of taking care of ourselves and nurturing our personal growth and well-being. Whether it is through setting goals and staying motivated in business, developing a strong support network of friends and family, or engaging in mindfulness and meditation practices, the key is to prioritise self-care and embrace every moment of life.

The most important lesson we can take away from this book is that life is short and precious, and it is up to us to make the most of every moment. By cultivating a positive mindset, seeking help and support when needed, and focusing on personal growth and development, we can create a fulfilling and meaningful life that is true to who we are. Let us continue to learn, grow, and embrace all that life has to offer.

Here are some action steps for readers to take after reading this book:

1. Reflect on your life.
Take some time to reflect on your life and identify areas where you need to make changes. Think about your values and what matters most to you.

2. Set goals.
Once you've identified areas where you want to make changes, set specific goals for yourself. Make sure your goals are realistic and achievable.

3. Develop a plan.
Create a plan for achieving your goals. Break down your goals into smaller steps and create a timeline for achieving each step.

4. Take action.

Start taking action towards your goals. Take small steps each day to work towards your goals.

5. Practice self-care.

Take care of yourself physically, emotionally, and mentally. This can include getting enough sleep, eating healthy, exercising, practising mindfulness, and seeking support when needed.

6. Build a support network.

Surround yourself with people who support and encourage you. Build relationships with friends, family, and professionals who can provide guidance and support.

7. Embrace uncertainty.

Learn to embrace uncertainty and view challenges as opportunities for growth and learning.

8. Seek help when needed.

If you are struggling with mental health issues or other challenges, seek help from a professional. Don't hesitate to reach out for support when you need it.

By taking these action steps, you can start living a more fulfilling life and achieving your goals. Remember, change takes time and effort, but it's worth it in the end.

Life is full of ups and downs. It presents us with many challenges that test our strength, resilience, and character. However, with the right mindset, attitude, and tools, we can overcome any obstacle and live a fulfilling life. This book has explored various topics ranging from personal development, self-improvement, relationships, health, and wellness, among others. It has highlighted the importance of developing a growth mindset, setting goals, and taking action to achieve them. It has also emphasised the need for self-care practices, such as mindfulness, exercise, and nutrition, to maintain physical and emotional well-being.

And that's a wrap...

So, you're probably having a bad day. If it wasn't for the risk of losing your freedom and the daily threat of backdoor penetration you may be thinking of doing some serious crimes. Well, let me try and cheer you up. One day, you will die... I've done it again. Let me explain. The average person lives 81 years which is approximately... A lot of fucking hours and you've spent some of those reading this so, now it's time to go fucking live it. Live your best life, nobody else's and to everyone who disagrees, just tell them to fuck off!

This book has shown that we can always learn and grow, no matter our circumstances or challenges. It has provided practical tips, tools, and resources to help us navigate life's challenges and make the most of every moment.

I hope I've turned a bad day around for you and thank you so much for reading. Make sure to follow me on my social media channels and I hope tomorrow is a better day.

Cheers.
That Ginger Fella

Printed in Great Britain
by Amazon

25777402R00078